# Script for Life

## In the Midst of the Chaos

Author

Gary Casale

# Copyright Page

**"Script for Life
In the Midst of the Chaos"**

All Bible quotations are based on the Authorized King James Version; a public domain document.

The Hebrew fonts used in this book were provided with permission by:

"Joy In The World"; Shippensburg, PA.

**ISBN-13:
978-1500884833**

**ISBN-10:
1500884839**

**Copyright 2017 by Gary Casale.
All rights reserved.
gar7cas@gmail.com**

# Dedication

This book is dedicated to my wonderful wife and helpmeet of 50 years, who stands by me in life and assisted me with editing the content of this book.

# Table of Contents

Pages 6-10                      Preface and Introduction

Pages 12-34        Hebrew Alphabet with Paleo Hebrew Letter Representations and Meaning

| Hebrew Words | English | Page Number |
|---|---|---|
| Palal | Pray | 38 |
| Leb | Heart | 40 |
| Batach | Trust | 42 |
| Shalom | Peace | 44 |
| Muth | Die / Death | 46 |
| Bariyth | House | 48 |
| Dabar | Word | 50 |
| Dalet | Door | 52 |
| Gan | Garden | 54 |
| Eden | Eden | 56 |
| Chen | Grace | 58 |
| Natsal | Deliver | 60 |
| Nahal | Guide | 62 |
| Niyr | Lamp | 64 |
| Lechem | Bread | 66 |
| Chay | Life | 68 |
| Halal | Praise | 70 |
| Pariy | Fruit | 72 |
| Biyn | Understanding | 74 |
| Ayin | Eye | 76 |
| Panayim | Presence / Face | 78 |
| Chokmah | Wisdom | 80 |
| Qowl | Voice | 82 |
| Yare' | Fear | 84 |
| Yalak | Walk | 86 |
| Derek | Way | 88 |
| Yada | Know | 90 |
| Chalal | Profane | 92 |
| Chata' | Sin | 94 |
| Salach | Forgive | 96 |
| Tiqvah | Hope | 98 |

| Hebrew Words | English | Page Number |
|---|---|---|
| Emeth | Truth | 100 |
| Ahab | Love | 102 |
| Ranan | Joy / Rejoice | 104 |
| Padah | Redeem | 106 |
| Yahshua | Salvation | 108 |
| Nabal | Foolish / Fool | 110 |
| Naqah | Free / Innocent | 112 |
| Aneg | Delight | 114 |
| Shama | Hear / Obey | 116 |
| Ruwach | Spirit | 118 |
| Yetser | Mind / Imagination | 120 |
| Nacham | Comfort | 122 |
| Kahal | Assembly / Congregation | 124 |
| Tahillah | Laudation / Praise | 126 |
| Kallah | Bride | 128 |
| Shemen | Oil / Shine | 130 |
| 'Owr | Light | 132 |
| Tsel | Shadow | 134 |
| Ra'ah | See | 136 |
| Towb | Good / Goodness | 138 |
| Hagah | Meditate / Imagine | 140 |
| Qavah | Wait / Patience | 142 |
| Zachar | Remember | 144 |
| Yachal | Wait / Hope | 146 |
| Cela | Rock / Fortress | 148 |
| Aman | Faithful / Believe | 150 |
| Tsedeq | Righteousness | 152 |
| Shed | Devil / Daemon | 154 |
| Sane | Hate / Enemy | 156 |
| Halak | Walk / Come | 158 |
| Anah | Answer / Hear | 160 |
| Pala | Miracle / Wonderful | 162 |
| Ta'ah | Error / Astray | 164 |
| Sheqer | Falsehood / False / Lies | 166 |
| Ra'ah | Shepherd / Feed / Pastor | 168 |
| Kuwl | Sustain / Nourish / Feed | 170 |
| Luwach | Table / Tablet | 172 |
| Chesed | Mercy | 174 |
| Edah | Witness / Testimony | 176 |

# **Preface**
## Script for Life
## In the Midst of the Chaos

My understanding and preparation for writing this book has been in development for many, many years. My early walk in faith started when I was encouraged to start reading the Bible by a believer named Ralph, who at the time was working, washing dishes at a bar. I bought the J.B. Phillips translation of the Bible and read it in its entirety, as he suggested. During my reading and shortly after completion, my life changed, and I was born again by the Word of God.

My interest in the Scriptures continued to grow over the years and has helped me to learn about life, faith and the reality the LORD has created for us to discover and to apply from His Word.

With all that being said, and without documenting my 1000 page testimony, my desire to know the Scriptures lead me to studying the Hebrew words found in the Bible. Through that study, I have come to realize that the Hebrew Scriptures (Tanach/Old Testament) are the dictionary for the "New Testament" Scriptures. One cannot fully understand the Bible without knowing the original meaning of the words, as they were intended to be understood, at the time they were written, prior to cultural influences.

Of course, most of the basic and fundamental

truths have survived over the ages and many believers are blessed by these truths.

During my study of Biblical Hebrew, I discovered ancient Paleo Hebrew. At first, when reading the words and individual Paleo letters, I thought that the letter pictures and word concepts were interesting and coincidental. After continued study and more analysis, I came to realize that the Paleo pictures found in the original ancient Paleo Hebrew words were full of meaning and not coincidental at all. I use this illustration: before I saw the text in "2D", but now, I see and understand the Scriptures in "3D".

You will also discover the prophetic nature, shadow types and truths that the words, and even the letters of Scripture portray. The pictorial imagery of the original letters, words and idioms, seen from a Hebraic perspective, are way beyond outstanding.

All the Words of Scripture are inspired for our understanding, revealing the reality and truths to harmonize our lives with the LORD and those around us. We need to transform our knowledge "about" the Scriptures, to knowing the "inspiration" and "implication" the Scriptures have on us. Then each one of us can develop the "application" to our individual lives. I developed a strong desire to share my studies and findings that the Christian faith is deep-rooted in the ancient Paleo Hebrew Words and was created for us since the beginning of time.

# Introduction

As you read this devotional, you will see the simple meaning and thought, yet depth of implication in the letters and the profound significance of the inspired Words found in the Scriptures. The letters of Scripture, originally drawn as sketches, images, or pictures, bring a very rich, prophetic and meaningful connotation of the written Word, as it was first presented thousands of years ago in Paleo Hebrew.

I will present each word and letter with the fundamental meaning of each letter and corresponding sketch or image. I will use the most basic meaning of each letter and will avoid the use of abstract inferences of the letter images. The letter pictures speak for themselves, in that the appearance of the representations describe the simple, yet profound narrative being communicated.

There is a continuity of thought presented within the 22 letter/pictures of the Hebrew alphabet. As you discover the words of this book, you will begin to see the scriptures in "3D", because of the original thought the letter depictions present to our understanding, sometimes hidden within the text. Contemplate and reflect on the words, images, letters and narrative presented in this devotional, to discover what the Script has to say about Life in the Midst of the Chaos.

As you read and contemplate the words, letters and related "depictions" illustrated in this devotional, you will be amazed at the depth and meaning of each word, the beauty of the Paleo Hebrew letters, and language with its integral relevance to the Scriptures. Paleo Hebrew is the original, (Early Semitic; Moses) ancient form of the Hebrew script and tongue. In addition to sharing the Paleo Hebrew pictorial meaning of each letter and associated words, I will place these words in association with some of your favorite verses in the Holy Scriptures.

Within each of the words selected for this first edition of "Script for Life, In the Midst of the Chaos", you will find the earliest meaning of each letter described in the original framework of the word. For each word a reflective narrative will be presented, referencing Scripture, unfolding the word associations consistent with the text, while harmonizing the Holy Scriptures. The individual Paleo Hebrew letters and corresponding images reveal and support the Gospel.

Also, some of the words and letter combinations are still being uncovered and understood from ancient scrolls and recent archeological findings. Some of the idioms of old remain unknown to us today. Yesterday "it was raining cats and dogs!" An idiom of today, probably not used thousands of years ago, would be an unknown concept, and would not be understood in some cultures. An ancient idiom, "coals of fire on the head", a puzzling concept in our culture today, was actually a blessing to the ancient world.  The word Blessing/Asher in the ancient Paleo Hebrew literally means "fire on the head".  This method of carrying burning coals of fire on one's head is unknown to most of the world today. Carrying burning coals around in a bowl/basket on the head, to be available for starting a fire for cooking or to get warm, was a very common practice.  When anyone provided a coal to someone, it was considered a blessing.  Can you imagine today, trying to start a fire from scratch, with no matches or lighter?

You will see how the "picture letters" and language brings out a layer of meaning in the text, corresponding to the original intent and the prophetic nature of the words, first drawn as sketches, pictures, and or images in Paleo Hebrew, thousands of years ago.

Keep these words and letters in your thoughts, speech and actions during the day.  Living with the seeds of thought in this devotional will bear fruit in your words and actions.  In doing this you will continue to grow in your understanding, wisdom and knowledge of the Scriptures.  The inspired Words of Scripture, made from the combination of letters, are Spirit and Life.

Through the individual letters of this text you will discover the basic themes in the Scriptures. They are truly a <u>Script for Life</u> to be lived out <u>In The Midst of the Chaos</u> around us.

# Script for Life

## In the Midst of the Chaos

# The Hebrew Alphabet in Paleo Format

This section of <u>Script for Life</u> provides you with a good introduction to the 22 letters of the Hebrew Alphabet, the Paleo pictures associated with each letter, and the suggested meaning for each letter image. This section, proceeding the individual words presented in the book, will help you to "see" and understand the deep meaning of each letter, in preparation for these same letters to be combined into the Words found in the Hebrew Scriptures. (Genesis – Malachi)

This section will also provide you with a reference to look back at, as needed, while reading the Paleo letters and words in the devotional pages of this book.

All of the letters illustrated are based on an ancient vision, a primitive viewpoint, or a very early understanding of the world during that time. While some of the words you will see are prophetic in nature and point to a future fulfillment, most of the words are very straightforward and elementary in meaning, still holding true today. After peeling off the cultural norms that have invaded our understanding of the "actual" world around us today, one will see the validity and original intent of the Paleo text written to communicate the profound reality of the real world we live in and find ourselves today ……… according to the original Scriptures .

# **Aleph**

Aleph

Ox
Strength
Power

The ALEPH is the 1st letter of the Hebrew alphabet. The picture of the Ox represents strength, power, might or something that exemplifies great potency.

The words you will discover with the ALEPH will show the intent of the letter to mean something that is strong. The word Father (Aleph, Bet) is a perfect example, containing the letter ALEPH, indicating the strength or power of the House. Scripturally, the Father is the strength of His house, and if you let him, yours as well.

Being the initial letter of the Alphabet (Aleph, Bet), ALEPH shows its power, primacy and position of importance as number One.

## **Bet**

Bet

House
Dwelling
Inside

The BET is the 2nd letter of the Hebrew alphabet. The picture represents a "Paleo" floor plan of a tent or house, where one would reside, a habitation to dwell, or a place to live inside.

The central features of the House throughout scripture are found when we are aware of the essence of living inside of His domain, with His design and being a part of His family.

The key to living in His presence and being a part of His creation is to learn about His reality, His truth, as it is found in His house. The basis of this word "House" is to live inside with Him. Dwell with Him inside of His house, as part of His family.

# **Gimmel**

Gimmel

<u>Camel</u>
Lift Up
Present

The GIMMEL is the 3rd letter of the Hebrew alphabet. The Paleo sketch, representing a camel's leg, signifies something that lifts up and/or carries something.

The essence and action of a bent camel's leg portrays the classic movement of the camel from a stooped position to a raised up or elevated position. When loading a camel with goods, or when one gets up on a camel, the camel is in the hunched position, then raises up.

The idea that the GIMMEL presents is a concept of lifting up, presenting, or carrying something. This is an ideal characteristic that can be witnessed with the camel's distinctive movement.

# **Dalet**

**Dalet**

**Door**
Entrance
Gate

The DALET is the 4th letter of the Hebrew alphabet. This Paleo picture of a door portrays an entrance or gate into a tent, building, fenced or walled area for entry to the interior.

The key function of a DALET is to provide an entrance to a dwelling. A fundamental thought found in the scripture is the idea of coming into the Father's house, the House of the LORD, through the door He provided.

The DALET, is the way, path and gate to His kingdom. Yahshua (Jesus), the Messiah, said that He was the door and Good Shepherd of the sheepfold. We enter through The Door into the Father's house.

# **Hey**

Hey

**Hands Raised**
Behold
Reveal

The HEY is the 5th letter of the Hebrew alphabet. The ancient drawing represents a person with hands and arms raised up in the air toward the heavens.

The depiction of a person holding both hands into the air expresses the desire of somebody reaching up to the LORD, beholding, seeking and praising the creator of the heavens.
By beholding we become changed.

We reveal the Spirit of the LORD, as we lift up our hands to Him, seek His face and make known His existence in our lives, first within ourselves and then to those who live around us.

# Vav

Vav

**Nail**
Connect
Secure

The VAV is the 6th letter of the Hebrew alphabet. The picture representation literally is that of a nail, hook, and/or a tent peg.

This graphic image illustrates something that connects one object to another. In the sanctuary the VAV connected the vail to the various parts of the tabernacle.

Also, the picture usage of the VAV is seen connecting, the Hebrew text within the letters, words and concepts in the scriptures.

Many words in the text illustrate the function of the VAV. A profound image of this picture is beholding the Messiah nailed to the tree with a VAV. "Heaven and earth" connected with a nail.

# **Zayin**

Zayin

Tool
Cut
Weapon

The ZAYIN is the 7th letter of the Hebrew alphabet. The drawing characterizes a type of crude hand tool or a makeshift weapon utilized in ancient times.

The usage of the ZAYIN in the scriptures illustrates an activity of carving or cutting. The purpose of etching or engraving is a function of the ZAYIN tool. The ZAYIN letter found in the word can be seen in various ways, such as in the context of planting something in the ground.

One can see a weapon, plow, or imprinting device, when the context of the script requires such a "tool" to be applied to the meaning of the word. Again the meaning emerges in context with the script.

# **Chet**

ח

Chet

**Wall**
Protect
Prevent

The CHET is the 8th letter of the Hebrew alphabet. The Paleo picture resembles a wall or a fence type structure.

The letter CHET can have opposite meanings, depending on its usage in the text. The concept of blocking or preventing can also be interpreted as protecting someone or something. The usage conditional with regard to what side of the wall one is experiencing in a given situation.

The essence of the letter will be inherent in the overall representation of the word and usage. We will see that the wall of protection is a factor in our walk with the LORD, as He blocks, prevents and protects our lives each day from those things where we need His shelter.

# Tet

Tet

**Basket**
Surround
Contain

The TET is the 9th letter of the Hebrew alphabet. The ancient sketch of a TET represents a basket or a container, when looking down into the basket with a view, top down.

The imagery of the TET portrays the concept of being surrounded by something. The use of the TET in scripture is found in words indicating something being encircled or enclosed. Being encompassed by various circumstances and surrounded by our environment is an everyday occurrence in life.

The key to comprehending the TET words is understanding what is in the basket and what is governing. Containment could be good for safety, but being controlled could be a negative.

# **Yod**

Yod

**Hand**
Create
Make

The YOD is the 10th letter of the Hebrew alphabet. The Paleo picture of the YOD is that of a hand on the arm. The YOD, found throughout scripture, simply means a hand.

The usage of YOD describes that of a working hand and signifies the hand that creates, makes or accomplishes. The hand or YOD ultimately is responsible for "doing" and getting results in a given place, for a given person, or at a given time.

A great example of this is seen throughout scripture where, "the Hand of the LORD" is identified, signifying the LORDS control over all things. The YOD exhibits His ultimate power. The Hand is the hand of creation and action.

# Kaf

Kaf

Palm
**Bless**
Give

The KAF is the 11th letter of the Hebrew alphabet. The Paleo drawing represents the open palm of a hand. The KAF in Hebrew literally means the palm of a hand, and unlike the working hand of the yod, KAF represents a picture of an open hand. .

You will see the KAF used throughout the text in words related to blessing, opening, or giving something to/for someone. The words where the letter KAF is found are very enriching and demonstrate the beauty of receiving an open hand from The LORD and from each other.

The essence of the open hand is seen as giving or blessing someone and is witnessed by the open hand pouring out the oil of blessing.

# **Lamed**

ל

Lamed

J

**Staff**
Shepherd
Leader

The LAMED is the 12th letter of the Hebrew alphabet. The graphic illustration of the LAMED is that of a shepherd's staff. This is a vivid depiction of the classic shepherd's staff used in ancient times.

The LAMED is a symbol of authority, a leader or a teacher. The imagery of the shepherd's staff signifies an icon of a shepherd in the field with his flock, leading, teaching and guiding.

We all look for direction in life and we seek leadership and an authority to follow. We need to follow the voice of the Good Shepherd for our guidance through the door into His sheepfold and pasture. His sheep hear His voice and will follow, wherever The Shepherd leads.

# Mem

Mem

Water
Chaos
Peoples

The MEM is the 13th letter of the Hebrew alphabet. The Paleo letter illustrates waves in a body of water. The MEM character connotes water, waves of water, "seas of people" and the chaos found in rough troubled waters.

Within a body of water, one can find it calm and peaceful or turbulent and chaotic. The usage of the MEM will be found evident within the context of the word it is used. Some words portray a peaceful and serene condition, while some words display chaos and turbulence. Chaos vs. life is contrasted in the words throughout the Scriptures.

The MEM picture sometimes denotes the waves of chaos that people encounter in life's "sea".

# **Nun**

Nun

Fish
Life
Activity

The NUN is the 14th letter of the Hebrew alphabet and portrays a sketch of a fish. The fish represents life, action, activity or a seed. A scientific microscopic picture today would compare this Paleo image to a human seed, a necessity to continue life and sustain existence.

NUN is all about life, being alive and being active in a very positive sense. The NUN fish, a picture of liveliness, is a perfect representation for the essence of vitality and life giving energy.

The key factor related to the NUN is found in many words interrelated to life. The life giving seed of the Word of the LORD is to enhance and provide vigor and a zeal for life. Unlike the Mem, relating to chaos, the Nun is all about life.

# Samach

Samach

Prop
Support
Depend

The SAMECH is the 15th letter of the Hebrew alphabet. The primeval SAMECH imitates a likeness to a brace used to provide support or to assist by propping something up. Another image that can be seen is the form of a thorn, used to guard, defend or hold back, as in a fence using thorns as the prop for safeguarding.

The words utilizing the SAMECH point out a dependence, a need of support, or the act of defending something. The SAMECH is typically used to lean against another object, to hold it up. Today the crutch is a modern day example of a supportive tool used for someone in need.

Providing support and holding people up is found in the Scriptures, as a means of showing love.

# Ayin

Ayin

**Eye**
See
Understand

The AYIN is the 16th letter of the Hebrew alphabet. The simple drawing of the AYIN, even in its common use today, can be visualized as an eyeball.......an eye to see and understand.

The fundamental meaning of the AYIN, obvious in the picture, is of an eye that can see or watch, providing the sense of vision to an individual. Taking AYIN to a deeper spiritual context, the eye provides understanding.

When seeing something, one can visualize what they see in a physical sense, but the AYIN can go beyond the physical realm to the spiritual dimension of reality, when seeing the world through His Word. The LORD wants us to have eyes to see and to know what we are seeing.

# Pey

Pey

**Mouth**
Speak
Voice

The PEY is the 17th letter of the Hebrew alphabet. The Paleo drawing expresses an outline of a mouth; an open mouth.

The very obvious meaning of the PEY, characterized by an open mouth, is conveying that someone is speaking. The mouth is revealed when a voice manifestation is heard.

All through scripture the usage of the PEY is quite apparent and can be seen in various words, where speaking or talking is evident.

The expression of the mouth, when open, can be seen uttering, and is witnessed with many types of vocalizations from a whisper to a scream. We use our voice to speak and always listen for His.

# **Tzadi**

Tzadi

**Hook**
Desire
Passion

The TZADI is the 18th letter of the Hebrew alphabet. The ancient picture looks like a hook type object. Some scholars identify this likeness to a fishhook.

The TZADI, as represented by the sketch, hooks something or someone physically. One can also be mentally hooked to something, expressing a feeling of passion or a strong desire for something they require or want.

The TZADI is a great representation of someone being in need, or in well-known terminology, someone that is "hooked". Being "hooked" to the right things can be a very positive experience, especially when one has a passion for the Truth found in The Word of God.

# Kof

Kof

**Back of Head**
Behind
Follow

The KOF is the 19th letter of the Hebrew alphabet. The drawing portrays an illustration of the back of a person's head or behind the head.

The concept of this picture is to render the meaning that something is behind you or something is following behind. Likewise, this sketch could also express that you are following something or someone. Following something could also be rendered as following something conceptually, as in following the scriptures.

An example is that of the Good Shepherd where His sheep follow Him and are behind Him.
His sheep hear His voice and they follow Him. We can follow physically and/or spiritually. We can leave something behind us or follow aptly.

# **Resh**

Resh

Head
Person
Thoughts

The RESH is the 20th letter of the Hebrew alphabet. It is a sketch of a person's head.

The representation of the RESH, the head, depicts a person, ones thoughts, the top, or the beginning. The individual meaning of the letter becomes obvious, as you interpret the meaning and context of the word in which the letter RESH is found.

The predominant usage of the RESH is found to mean a person or the thoughts of an individual. The person we are comes from the feelings and beliefs in our head.

Our head, comprising our thoughts, represents and defines us as individuals, and reveals us.

# Shin

Shin

Teeth
Consume
Destroy

The SHIN is the 21st letter of the Hebrew alphabet. This letter bears a resemblance to teeth, as illustrated in the picture letter.

The usage of this letter can especially be witnessed in its primitive context, where the sharp teeth of an animal can be imagined biting and piercing its prey. The meaning of the SHIN emerges with teeth biting and penetrating, while in the process of destroying.

The other meaning that emerges from the SHIN is that of consuming something. In a spiritual sense, consuming can be a positive or a negative, depending on what is consuming you. To be consumed by The LORD is a very positive state of being.

# **Tav**

Tav

Cross
Sign
Covenant

The TAV is the 22nd and last letter of the Hebrew alphabet. The ancient drawing is that of a cross.

The TAV is an indicator of a mark, a sign, or a sign of a covenant. This mark, as illustrated by a cross type symbol, carries with it, in every word it is found, an indicator of something identified as sealed, marked, or an agreement of covenant. In modern times, when we agree to a covenant contract, we sign at the "X", on the bottom line.

The TAV throughout the scriptures takes on the significance of a sign. The TAV symbol of the cross, created thousands of years ago, was an ancient prophecy of the ultimate covenant sign given to mankind for us to identify and realize. This is clearly the sign of the New Covenant.

## DEVOTIONAL

Here is the word format you will find in the <u>Script for Life</u> Devotional:

Each Hebrew word and the English word as used in the text will be displayed. The Modern Hebrew letters will be presented. The name of each Hebrew letter will be identified. The ancient Paleo script will be characterized for each letter. The meaning of each letter and the interpretation of the combined word pictures / letters will be presented.

Before we get to the main section, here is a sample of a familiar word, utilizing the Paleo concepts of everyday life known to mankind thousands of years ago.

| | | |
|---|---|---|
| English / Hebrew Words → | **Father** **Ab** | |
| Modern Hebrew Script → | ב | א |
| | Bet | Aleph |
| Paleo Script → | ⌑ | ⛦ |
| Paleo Meaning → | <u>House</u> Dwelling Inside | <u>Ox</u> Power Strength |
| Paleo Picture Meaning → | **Strength in The House** **The Power of The House** | |

# Morning
# Boker

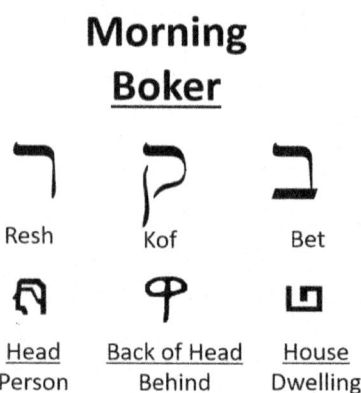

| Resh | Kof | Bet |
|---|---|---|
| Head | Back of Head | House |
| Person | Behind | Dwelling |

## The House Behind the Person

The above is an example of how this devotional will be presented. Have you ever heard the greeting, "Boker Tov"? This means Good Morning in Hebrew! Three letters make up the word BOKER in the Hebrew: A Bet, a Kof, and a Resh. Notice that Hebrew is read from right to left.

While this devotional is not a study per se of the Hebrew language. I will follow the structure and meaning, as documented in the biblical lexicons and concordances that are available and can be referenced very easily. I will not be commenting on the vowels, verb tenses, adjectives, adverbs or any of the other rudiments in a typical language study.

This book is for devotional purposes and your enjoyment, not for a degree in Biblical Hebrew.

Please reference the illustration on the previous page to see the combined meaning of the word pictures, as represented by each Paleo letter/script.

The BET is illustrated in the Paleo as a house, and "pictures": a house, in or being inside, etc.

The KOF is illustrated in the Paleo as the back of a person's head, and "pictures": behind, follows, following, etc.

The RESH is illustrated in the Paleo as a person's head/person, and "pictures": a person, a head, a man, an individual, etc.

The meaning of the combination of the three word pictures, BET - house, KOF - behind, and RESH – man = House Behind Man. The house is behind a person. In the morning, the house is behind you! A perfect picture of the word "morning"! When you leave for the day in the morning, your house is behind you.

  My purpose in this devotional is to assist you in your daily walk with the LORD, through the words and letters of the script, while enhancing your biblical understanding and desire for the text. As you embark on your journey through this devotional, it is the start of a new day........ and remember: a picture is worth 1000 words, one letter and one word at a time.

        Boker Tov!!!   Good Morning!!!

# Pray
## Palal

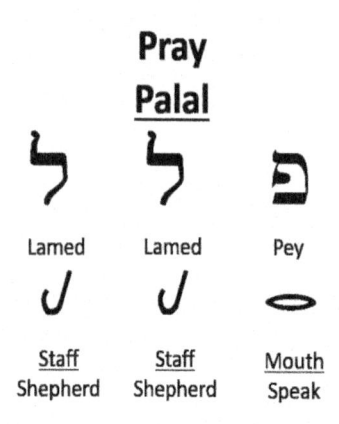

| ל | ל | פ |
|---|---|---|
| Lamed | Lamed | Pey |
| ⌒ | ⌒ | ⌀ |
| Staff Shepherd | Staff Shepherd | Mouth Speak |

## Speak to The Shepherd of Shepherds

Ps 5:2 Hearken unto the voice of my cry, my King, and my God: for unto thee will I pray.

To begin this devotional, I chose the word "Pray", a word that is very well known by everyone and is intrinsically associated with devotion.

The root word "Palal" means pray in Hebrew. It is fitting to contemplate this word while we begin our journey into this devotional, as the word "pray" is fundamental to the scriptures and is vital in seeking His presence and direction in our lives.

When not conversing with others, endeavor to spend additional time talking with Him and engage Him more when "talking" to ourselves. In so doing, we will hear from Him, while we anticipate and listen for His voice speaking to our hearts. This is one way we can enter into a closer relationship with Him and realize His companionship with us.

Speaking to the Shepherd of shepherds is found throughout the Scriptures as a means of engagement with the LORD in our everyday lives. We need not wait for major events to take place to include Him in our daily thoughts, words and decisions. He is willing to engage us each moment, during the conversations of our day with Him. Embrace each day, moment by moment, in consultation with The Shepherd of shepherds. In doing this, you will seek His face or presence in all things in your daily walk. (Ps 27:8; 105:4)

The key to prayer is living each moment in His presence and inviting Him in on the conversation you are having with life. Consciously and purposely connect with Him as you think and contemplate your thoughts, words and actions.

It is reassuring for us to know, when we direct our thoughts toward Him and converse with Him, we will experience the Spirit of His presence. We will recognize His words and The Good Shepherd will guide and direct us, as He guides His Sheep. So speak to the Shepherd of shepherds in your daily walk and stay connected to Him.

1Thes 5:17 Pray without ceasing.

# Heart
# Leb

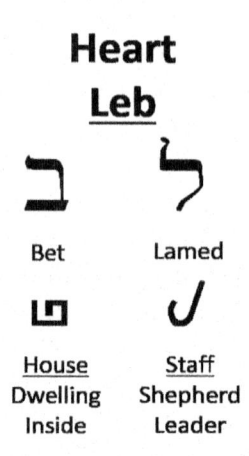

| ב | ל |
|---|---|
| Bet | Lamed |
| 🏠 | 𐤋 |
| **House** | **Staff** |
| Dwelling | Shepherd |
| Inside | Leader |

## The Shepherd of the House

Ps 119:11   Thy word have I hid in mine <u>heart</u>, that I might not sin against thee.

We hear many voices and evaluate many thoughts that come our way in our day to day experience.  The Shepherd of our House is the voice of authority we follow in our lives.  We respond to the Shepherd that has the authority of our heart.  It is to this authority we give our lives to guide us with the decisions we make each day.  Who is the Shepherd of your house?

We invite the LORD to dwell in our hearts and to live in us.  When His Word, the bread of life, is hid in our hearts, we make decisions based on instructions on the tables of our heart and we become living epistles, following the Shepherd of the house where we live and dwell.  When we seek His presence in our lives and look to Him in everything we do, He will fortify us, shield us, and bless us with His mercy and grace. Staying connected to Him is the key to walking with Him.

With Him as the Authority, we will find truth, and as we walk in truth, we will find freedom, since His teachings set us free. His words, the light of life will shine from our hearts, as we make Him manifest ..... The Shepherd and Guide of our lives.

He is our God and we are the people of His pasture and the sheep of His hand. (Ps 95:7) We rejoice when we make the LORD, the Good Shepherd, the authority of our house, at home in our hearts.

In all aspects of life, deep inside our souls, we anticipate, calculate, evaluate, and contemplate thoughts and actions that impact our lives and the lives of others. "From the bottom of our hearts" (a modern idiom we hear today) we confirm our beliefs and decisions, based on the spirit of the shepherd that has the authority over our lives, whether we do it knowingly or not. The key is to have the Words of the Good Shepherd hid in our being to access, as a foundation for everything we say, think and do, in pursuing life.

2Cor 3:3 Forasmuch as ye are manifestly declared to be the epistle of Christ ministered by us, written not with ink, but with the Spirit of the living God; not in tables of stone, but in the fleshly tables of the heart.

# Trust
## Batach

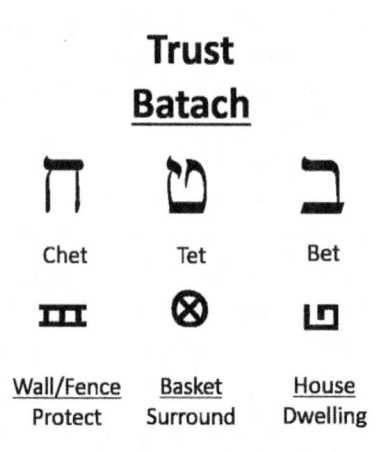

| ח | ט | ב |
|---|---|---|
| Chet | Tet | Bet |
| ⅲ | ⊗ | ഥ |
| Wall/Fence | Basket | House |
| Protect | Surround | Dwelling |

## House Surrounded and Protected

Prov 3:5-6   Trust in the LORD with all thine heart; and lean not unto thine own understanding.  In all thy ways acknowledge Him, and he shall direct thy paths.

When we enter into His house and reside with Him, we are surrounded and protected.  When we choose to dwell in His house, we are choosing to abide in Him and honor His desires.

We trust everything that He says and does.  We follow His ways and depend on Him for all outcomes.  In our Father's house we are safe and sound!   As we seek to understand His creation and how creation was designed, our paths will be directed by Him.

In His Word we discover His house, His creation, His laws that govern all aspects of life, and His plan to sustain life throughout His universe. By coming to trust Him, we recognize that we choose to enter into relationship with Him and that relationship is found inside His house.

We are no longer strangers on this earth, but are fellow citizens with the saints and of the household of God. (Eph2:19) Being of God's household, we follow the principles that He has established, as valid truths to govern our lives. We find true freedom when living in His house, through trusting in Him and following his Word. He created all things with His Word and through the Truth of His Word He sets us free.

We come into His house through the front door, the Word of God. By following His Word as a guide to our lives, we live inside of the Father's house and become part of the household of faith, a faith that comes by hearing, and hearing by the Word of God. (Rom 10:17) Our faith becomes the evidence of our trust in Him, as we walk in His word through the valleys and mountain tops of life.

In Him we are secure, for inside of His house we find shelter, direction and abundant life. By responding to His call to enter, we find refuge, purpose and confidence for the future. Yes, in His House, we are Surrounded and Protected.

(Rom 8:28) And we know that all things work together for good to them that love God, to them who are the called according to His purpose.

# Peace
## Shalom

| Mem | Vav | Lamed | Shin |
|---|---|---|---|
| Water | Nail | Staff | Teeth |
| Chaos | Connect | Authority | Destroy |

## Destroy the Authority Connected to Chaos

Isa 26:3   Thou wilt keep him in perfect peace, whose mind is stayed on thee: because he trusteth in thee.

Peace comes to us when we let God rule in our hearts, and when we choose God's Word, the Gospel of Peace, to direct our decisions.  We observe the turmoil on this earth, because the philosophies of mankind have enticed us to follow the ways and authority of man, while ignoring the "way, truth and the life" God has outlined for us.  Instead of Peace, "dead ends, lies, and chaos" are experienced by mankind, because we do not trust in Him, do not follow His Word and we prioritize the "wisdom" of man.

In John 16:33, the Lord told us that in Him we would have peace and in the world there would be tribulation (chaos).

The heavenly host was praising God when the Messiah was born, because He will bring peace on earth and good will toward men. (Luke 2:12-14) Until the shepherd and authority of chaos, Satan, is finally eliminated, we will not see peace completely restored on this earth.

In anticipation of that occasion, we need to give the authority of our lives to the "Prince of Peace", The Shepherd of shepherds, as we hear His voice and follow Him into His sheepfold. (Isa 9:6; John 10:3-5)

As more and more individuals come into harmony with His Word, being The Authority, the more we will observe peace on earth and realize the true meaning of the Word. When we see "the destruction of the authority connected to chaos" replaced by His Authority in our culture and world, we will experience the true Peace the Lord talked about! (John 14:27)

Chaos inevitably develops when the shepherd and authority not in harmony with God's Word is allowed to exist. As we give our thoughts, words and actions to the LORD, as a living sacrifice, we will begin to experience the peace He designed. As we are transformed by the renewing of our minds, we will experience more peace, proving THE Shepherd's will. (Rom 12)

Col 3:15   And let the peace of God rule in your hearts, to which also ye are called in one body; and be ye thankful.

# Death / Die
# <u>Muth</u>

| ת | ו | מ |
|---|---|---|
| Tav | Vav | Mem |
| † | Y | ∿∿ |
| <u>Cross</u> | <u>Nail</u> | <u>Water</u> |
| Covenant | Connect | Chaos |

## Chaos Connected to a Covenant

Gen 2:17  But of the tree of the knowledge of good and evil, thou shall not eat of it: for in the day that thou eatest thereof, thou shalt surely <u>die</u>.

This instruction from the LORD God, "not to eat from the tree of the knowledge of good and evil", was given to Adam in the garden as one of His first commandments regarding life and death on this earth.  Upon disobeying the LORD, Adam and Eve did not die immediately, but entered into a covenant of chaos.  This chaos covenant would begin a chain reaction of events, introducing entropy and physical death to mankind, while diminishing peace.

We can see the impact of this "knowledge" that they pursued and the turmoil in human history, resulting in the tragedies of our day.

Only by understanding and following His Words of Life can we neutralize to some degree the chaos we see around us for now. What we are experiencing today is not His design. His design was life eternal with no chaos or disorder.

Chaos and ultimate death is the exact opposite of what God intended for us and His creation. The tree mixed with the knowledge of good and evil was not to be a source of "food" for man to eat. As the Creator, He knows what we should be "consuming" and what is best for us.
He desires that we look only to Him for knowledge re: life. It is through His instructions and by entering into covenant with Him that we find abundant life, peace and life eternal.

The Words of His teachings nourish us, bringing the joy and the rejoicing of eternal life into our hearts. (Jer 15:16; John 14:26-27) Let us seek for the covenant that comes from His instructions and find the sustenance to improve life, minimizing and eliminating the covenant of chaos, where possible, in this world.

What a beautiful kingdom he has planned for us. Peace without war, health without disease and life without death. We will understand the cause and effect of choosing anything that is not of His will. The covenant of chaos will not be desired, because the covenant of life will be confirmed.

1 Cor 15:22   For as in Adam all die, even so in Christ shall all be made alive.

## House
## Bariyth

| ת | י | ב |
|---|---|---|
| Tav | Yod | Bet |
| † | ‍↲ | ⌂ |
| Cross | Hand | House |
| Covenant | Create | Dwelling |

## House Created for The Covenant

Ps 23:6 Surely goodness and mercy shall follow me all the days of my life: and I will dwell in the house of the LORD forever.

The Lord's House is a spiritual House of Covenant with Him. He invites us to enter into His House, to be at home with Him. When we enter and live in His kingdom, He desires us to honor and obey His Words. (John 14:23-24) His mercy is everlasting to those who keep His Covenant and remember His commandments. (Ps 103:17-19; Deut 4:13)

As the Creator of all things, He arranged the universe to function without chaos, when it operates in accord with His blueprint. To the extent chaos or entropy is found on this earth, something is out of harmony with His design. His House of Covenant is His perfect reality.

We find many houses mentioned in scripture; the house of bondage, house of the wicked, house of Pharaoh, house of Jacob, house of Israel, and the house of God, etc. There are many spiritual houses to enter. We must understand the character of all houses inviting us to come inside and build our lives upon.   (Prov 3:33; Mat 7:24)

Before we open the door to cross the threshold and abide in any house, we need to make sure that the dwelling is in accord with our Father and we must hear if the words are in agreement with our Father's purpose, a covenant with life, not with chaos.

Our Father's creation is the House He made for us, and all existing entities, to experience and to enjoy life without pain or suffering.  His design is one of serenity and tranquility for all.  The Covenant House is that place He made where we find our way back home.  Through His Covenant, we and all creation, discover His eternal plan and sign (tav), as an everlasting reminder of the sacrifice He made in our behalf. In His home we find His Covenant and heart.

When we choose to be in covenant with Him, we come home to Him inside His House, The House Created for The Covenant.

Heb 3:6  But Christ as a Son over His own house; whose house are we, if we hold fast the confidence and the rejoicing of the hope firm to the end.

# Word
## Dabar

| ר | ב | ד |
|---|---|---|
| Resh | Bet | Dalet |

&lt; Son : Bar &gt;

| Head | House | Door |
|---|---|---|
| Man | Dwelling | Entrance |

## The Door of The Son

Ps 33:6  By the <u>Word</u> of the LORD were the heavens made and all the host of them by the breath of His mouth.

The Door into the Father's House is through His Word, His Son.  His Son is the Door established by the Father for entrance into His House; the Door of The Son.  In His Word we find access to His creation, into His House, through His Door. We know that we are in the Father's house when we come in through the correct door, His Word, the only entrance, the Holy Scriptures.

His Words reveal the voice of life, the Way, the Truth and the Life. (John 14:6) As we study the Scriptures, we find the roadmap for living now and see the master plan of eternal life in God's House in His creation and His design.  His reality is truth: He created the universe by His Word.

His Words give us the instructions on how to live and the light to see the correct path, as His Words are Spirit and His Words are life. (Ps 119:105; John 6:63b) We live not by bread alone, but by every Word that comes from the mouth of God, the Bread of life. (Mat 4:4) By "eating" His words we find life and experience the truth and reality of our existence. We not only need physical food to live, but also spiritual food as well, because we live in both a physical and spiritual dimension of being.

The thoughts of our Father in Heaven are expressed through the Words of His only begotten Son, the Messiah. His Words give us strength and purpose, as we live out His design and witness to His House of grandeur and glory.

While He prepares a place for us in the Father's house, we grow in faith and enter His Kingdom by hearing and following His Words revealed at the door. (John 14:1-4; Rom 10:17) The House is entered when we live in Him, His Word. The only Door to the Father's House is via the Words of His Son, Jesus, Yahshua the Messiah; The Door of The Son; The Word of God. We need to live in His Word, the Creator of all things.

John 1:1,3,14a In the beginning was the Word, and the Word was with God, and the Word was God. All things were made by him; and without Him was not any thing made that was made. And the Word was made flesh, and dwelt among us.....

## Door / Gate
## Dalet

| ת | ל | ד |
|---|---|---|
| Tav | Lamed | Dalet |
| † | ∪ | ⊤ |
| Cross | Staff | Door |
| Covenant | Shepherd | Entrance |

## Door of The Shepherd's Covenant

Prov 8:34, 35  Blessed is the man that heareth me, watching daily at my gates, waiting at the posts of my doors.  For whoso findeth me findeth life, and shall obtain favor of the LORD.

We come into the Father's House, the people of His pasture and the sheep of His hand (Ps 95:7), through Jesus (Yahshua), the Door (Gate) of the Shepherd, as we hear His voice.

To enter the House, His sheepfold, one must come in through the door/gate.  Entering through the door means to enter His domain through Him, through His Word.  His Word is the "Door of the Son."  We know that we are at the right house when we recognize the gateway of our Father's domain.  Are the words at the doorway in agreement with the Holy Scriptures?  Are the words consistent with the theology of the Bible?

Are the words, words of life, or are they words that advance chaos, when evaluating the character and spirit of that household? The gate to His kingdom leads unto life, as He intended it to be, with peace and without chaos.

As we listen to His Word and follow His Voice, we come into fellowship with Him, as a resident of His House. We, His sheep, hear His Voice and follow Him wherever he goes, for His Words are Spirit and they are life. He has the Words of eternal life. (John 6:63, 68)

The House He created represents His original and unique design for life. We come into covenant with the Shepherd, when we identify Him as LORD of our lives and follow His ways. We understand that His ways are for our benefit and His blessings are waiting for our realization.

There are many doors, gates and entrances to the various kingdoms on this earth, but we seek the residence of the True Shepherd and enter the door that he has provided for us. It is now apparent; the Door we choose to go through is the Door of The Shepherd and it is established on His Words and the terms of His Covenant. The Father's Son is the Door of life by His Word.

John 10:7, 9 Then said Jesus unto them again, Verily, verily, I say unto you, I am the door of the sheep. I am the door: by me if any man enter in, he shall be saved, and shall go in and out, and find pasture.

# Garden
## Gan

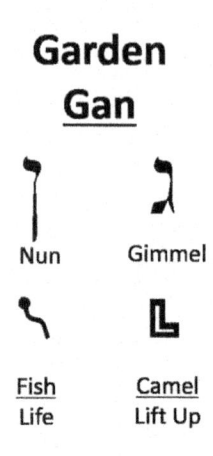

ן  ג

Nun  Gimmel

ᒐ    L

Fish  Camel
Life  Lift Up

## Lift up Life

Gen 2:15 And the LORD God took the man, and put him into the <u>garden</u> of Eden to dress it and to keep it.

The Garden of Eden is the place God made for mankind and His creation to begin life on this planet. It was a place where life was to be lifted up and respected. He established a set of basic principles for mankind to guard and maintain. In the Garden Adam and Eve had access to eat from the Tree of Life to enjoy existence on the earth forever and ever.

God's plan was for life to be fruitful, abundant, beautiful, and eternal. One stipulation was placed upon Adam and Eve to honor, in order for them to experience the reality of eternal life without incident. This instruction was not to eat fruit from the "tree of the knowledge of good and evil", or they would enter into a covenant of chaos; i.e. death. (Gen 2:7)

In guarding the LORD's requests, mankind was not to deviate from His instructions, pursuing life outside of His will, and was not to think that He was holding back any of life's blessings. Doubting the LORD and believing a lie, Adam and Eve sinned by following the deceiver's words, regarding the words of death, above the Words of life. (Gen 3:4-6) They were enticed by lust, naive desire and pride, thinking that these things were better than what the Father was giving to them. The Father is looking for those who want to do His will, follow Him, pursue life and not love the things of this world above Him. (1 John 2:14-17)

We lift up life by living our lives in Him, the gift of life, as He designed. The Garden of life will be restored and experienced when all of us follow His plan, the Words of life, written by the "Gardener" of all things.

Note: a garden was the place where death was introduced to the world. A garden was also used to expose death and lift up life for us to see. Yahshua's life was lifted up and resurrected in the garden for us to see His promise of life.

John 19:41 Now in the place where he was crucified there was a garden; and in the garden a new sepulchre, wherein was never man yet laid.

# Eden
## Eden

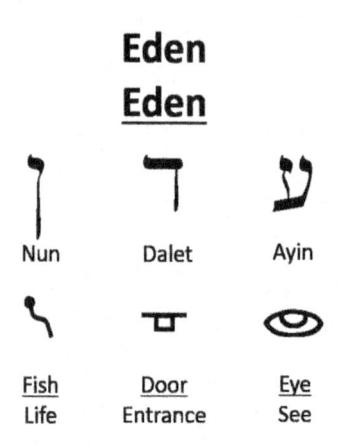

| Nun | Dalet | Ayin |
|---|---|---|
| Fish | Door | Eye |
| Life | Entrance | See |

## See/Understand the Door to Life

Gen 2:15 And the LORD God took the man, and put him into the garden of Eden to dress it and to keep it.

We see the door to life in the Garden of Eden, where God established creation and humankind. The framework was perfect, the entre' to life, an existence of health, a life of beauty, in an atmosphere of peace. No chaos existed inside the entrance of the house He created for the purpose of living a complete and full life.

Adam's responsibility was to dress the garden and to keep it, so the garden would flourish. He was to be the husbandman of Eden, an assignment given to Adam to work the garden of life, such that it would continue to thrive and bear much fruit. The other related responsibility given to him was to keep the garden, meaning to protect it from any form of chaos. His role was to nurture and to guard life within the setting, facilitating what was created for mankind to flourish and to experience life as originally designed.

Eden pictures a place where true life in its original design is found, and it is interesting to see, within the word Eden, that we enter the Garden of Eden through the door. Yahshua (Jesus) said, to find an abundant life, He is the door to enter. (John 10:9-10) For mankind to return to the Eden condition, we must enter through the door and wait for the promise of the new earth to be re-created. (Rev 21:1-4)

What a beautiful experience it will be for mankind to realize Eden again. The choices of mankind will be in support of life and not choices that advance death, the covenant of chaos. A life of blessing and not curses will be the only reality. Hate, famine, war, sickness, death, etc., will not be found in the Garden of Eden.

As our faith grows, we will see and desire life inside the door to Eden. The only way to eternal life is through the door to our Father's garden.

Gen 3: 22b, 24 and now, lest he put forth his hand, and take also of the tree of life, and eat, and live forever: So he drove out the man; and he placed at the east of the garden of Eden Cherubims, and a flaming sword which turned every way, to keep the way of the tree of life.

# Grace
## Chen

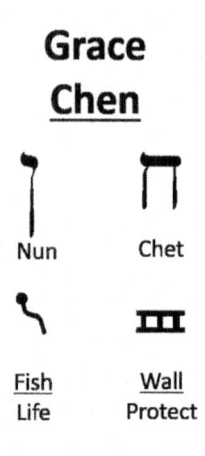

| Nun | Chet |
|---|---|
| Fish | Wall |
| Life | Protect |

## Protect Life

Gen 6:8    But Noah found <u>grace</u> in the eyes of the LORD.

Grace, God's gift to us, has always been the hallmark of YHVH. His whole revelation to us has been about protecting life and helping us to see the value of life. Opposed to this characteristic of the LORD is the destruction or devaluation of life and the instigation of chaos.

Noah found grace in the eyes of the LORD (Gen 6:8-9) at a time when mankind was focused on creating chaos upon chaos. In order to protect life, as mankind was bent upon evil, the LORD needed to start over with those who respected His words and walked with Him. His Creation is all about life; abundant with a thriving reality.

The LORD's purpose is, and always was, to

guard life and provide for a fruitful, everlasting life. In preparation for His kingdom, while we wait for Him to return, He wants us to be in harmony with His desire to guard and keep life consistent with His design. His vital instructions about living in this universe supports life and reveals the chaos to be avoided.

God's focus has always been about life and His desire to save us by His grace, thus providing us the motivation to magnify life, by living in covenant with Him. When walking in covenant with Him, we assist Him in representing the will of His kingdom on earth, as it is in heaven. (Mat 6:10)

Upon discovering grace, we are motivated to desire His will and bring Him praise and honor in all that we do, not due to obligation or requirement, but because we realize what He has done for us and His Words are now written in our hearts. He is our God, we are His people. (Jer 31:33-34) We want to live according to His plan for life, for by grace He died to rescue us.

So upon receiving grace, the gift of God through faith, we become new creatures, His workmanship, created in Him unto good works, walking in such a manner that protects life and supporting the very reason why he died for us. (Eph 2:8-10) His ultimate will is to protect life.

Titus 2:11 For the grace of God that bringeth salvation hath appeared to all men.

## Deliver
## Natsal

| ל | צ | נ |
|---|---|---|
| Lamed | Tzadi | Nun |

| Staff | Hook | Fish |
|---|---|---|
| Shepherd | Desire | Life |

## Life Hooked to The Shepherd

Ps 25:20  O keep my soul, and <u>deliver</u> me: let me not be ashamed; for I put my trust in thee.

When we have our passions devoted to Him we are rescued from death and are liberated from the chaos around us.  Our lives find true freedom in Him when we are absorbed and practice the words of the Shepherd.  Thus, when our lives are "hooked" to Him, we enter into His sheepfold, find pasture with Him, graze in His field, eat His food, come under His protection, and are liberated by His voice of life.

It is interesting to note that the word *"shadow"* is found within the word Natsal.  Tzadi + Lamed means shadow; hooked to the Shepherd.  In order to have a shadow there must be light and an object to produce a shadow.  As we dwell close to Him in His presence, trusting the

Shepherd, we find refuge and sanctuary in His shadow. (Ps 91:1-2) Staying close to Him, and living as it were, in His shadow, is a very safe place to experience life.

The light of His words, the voice of the Shepherd, preserve us and point us in the direction to follow unto the coming of the new heavens and new earth. (2 Tim 4:18) We can now live life by trusting Him, without the fear of the eternal bondage of death, and experience the rescue of our souls, being "hooked" to Him now, as we wait, and ultimately when he returns for the final rescue. (Heb 2:13-15)

Stay close to Him and live in His presence, in conscious awareness of Him, as much as possible, and you will find your life hooked to the Shepherd, living with Him, delivered from the cares of this world and chaos that surrounds us. We can trust Him for our lives now and forever.

We can experience life, like we have never experienced it before, as being joined to Him is life now and life eternal. We find deliverance from death and avoid the traps of this world when our lives are "hooked" to the Shepherd. Experience the rescue and be blessed forever.

Gal 1:3-4  Grace be to you and peace from God the Father, and from our Lord Jesus Christ, who gave himself for our sins, that He might deliver us from this present evil world, according to the will of God and our Father.

## Guide
## <u>Nahal</u>

| ל | ה | נ |
|---|---|---|
| Lamed | Hey | Nun |
| 𐤋 | 𐤄 | 𐤍 |
| <u>Staff</u> | <u>Hands Raised</u> | <u>Fish</u> |
| Shepherd | Beholding | Life |

## Life Beholding The Shepherd

Ps 31:3  For thou art my rock and my fortress; therefore for thy name's sake lead me, and <u>guide</u> me.

We find guidance when we behold and follow the Shepherd.  For now, we behold Him through His Words, His Father's Words and the Spirit of Truth, found in the Holy Scriptures.  As we behold His Words, the Words of Spirit and life, and apply them, we become changed, finding true liberty and freedom in this life.  (2Cor 3:17; John 6:63)

Because there are so many distractions encountered in this world, we need to be reflecting on His ways, for He is the Way, the Truth and the Life.  (John 14:6)  The more we come into harmony with His Truths, the realities of life, the more we will want to follow His leadership, as the Guide of our lives. By beholding Him we become changed and grow into His "image" by His Spirit. We are guided by Him and will be a witness to the Gospel, as we walk in His Light. (2 Cor 3:18-4:4) He said, when the Spirit of Truth is come, He would guide us into all Truth, and the Truth would Guide us to a life glorifying the Shepherd. (John 16:13-14)

The enemy has come to lead us away from the Shepherd into chaos, by distracting us from beholding that which brings true life and peace. While we focus on the Shepherd, we will realize life to the fullest with Him as our Guide, protecting and sustaining our lives. We will mature into a deeper understanding of Him, knowing His desire for us is to have an abundant life. Abundant life is found in Him, guided by Him, as we behold Him in this life. (John 10:10)

Life beholding the Shepherd develops into life revealing the Shepherd. The more we are focused on the Shepherd, the more we will be guided by His Spirit, and the more we will be allowing the Spirit to live inside of us, leading us each step of the way. We will be able to say that the Shepherd leads and guides us beside the still waters. (Ps 23:2b)

John 16:13 Howbeit when he, the Spirit of Truth, is come, he will guide you into all truth: for he shall not speak of himself; but whatsoever he shall hear, that shall he speak: and he will shew you things to come.

# Lamp
## Niyr

| Resh | Yod | Nun |
|---|---|---|
| Head | Hand | Fish |
| Think | Do | Life |

## Life to the Hand and Head

Ps 119:105 NUN. Thy word is a <u>lamp</u> unto my feet, and a light unto my path.

We find life in God's Word and that life is demonstrated in what we think and do. The thoughts of our head formulate into actions. Thoughts + Words + Action = Life. The lamp provides light to our journey in the form of guidance along the pathway of life. When encountering darkness along the way, the candle will illuminate the path our steps should take, with the light of the lamp. (Psalm 119:130)

When we follow His Word we will not walk in darkness, as He is the Light of the world and in Him we find the Way, the Truth, and the Life. His instructions, our lamp, provide the basis for thought, the Way of life, and will lead us step by step. (John 14:5-6; Prove 6:23)

As we behold Him and He lives in us, we will illuminate our candles, bringing glory to our Father in heaven. (Mat 5:14-16) He will guide us through the darkness and will keep our candles lit, as we seek out His Word and trust in Him. (Psalm 18: 28)

To have the Light of Life is to follow Him, to walk in the Light, and not in the darkness. (John 8:12) As we live in His Word, we experience salvation, and we eliminate the fears caused by the darkness. (Psalm 27:1; 1Peter 2:9)
As we apply the principles of God's Word, The Lamp of our lives, we walk as children of light. (Eph 5:8) The experience we have and share brings light to others, when we reveal the lamp through our thoughts and actions.

Take the lamp with you wherever you go. Light is the ultimate power in this world for us to accomplish anything of any substance and value. Whether we do anything physically to see, or we do anything mentally with our brains to understand, we need "light". The Word of God is that lamp which provides the light to see the reality that is in our path. Life to our hands and head is a gift from God found in His Word.

Mat 5:15-16 Neither do men light a candle, and put it under a bushel, but on a candlestick; and it giveth light unto all that are in the house. Let your light so shine before men, that they may see your good works, and glorify your Father which is in heaven.

# Bread
## Lechem

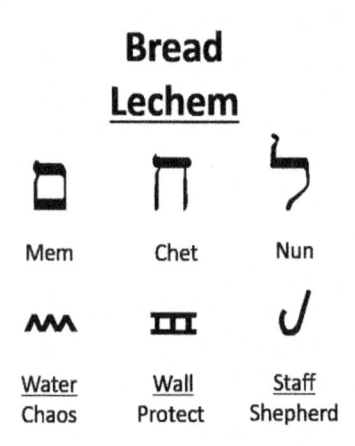

| מ | ח | ל |
|---|---|---|
| Mem | Chet | Nun |
| 〰 | ☷ | ʋ |
| Water<br>Chaos | Wall<br>Protect | Staff<br>Shepherd |

## Shepherd's Protection from Chaos

Ex 16:15 And when the children of Israel saw it, they said one to another, It is manna, for they wist not what it was. And Moses said unto them, This is the bread which the LORD hath given you to eat.

The bread from heaven is that bread provided by the shepherd to protect us from chaos. Jesus (Yahshua), the Word of God, became flesh and lived among us, the bread of life, for us to consume. When we eat His bread we are informed about the disorder around us. He is the Word of God (John 1:14), the bread we need to eat for life now and life eternal. We need physical food to live and thrive. So much more do we need spiritual food to exist and strengthen our hearts and lives. (John 6:35)

The bread that comes from heaven is that bread

providing us wisdom with understanding and helps us to relinquish the chaos in the world. (Prov 9:1-6) With understanding, we build what enhances life and impedes foolish atrophy.

Throughout scripture the living bread is represented by unleavened bread; bread without yeast or fermentation, now to be remembered as the prophetic realization of the body/bread and blood/wine of the Passover lamb, our Messiah. (Deut 16:2-3; Luke 22:19)

Upon eating His Word, our spiritual bread, we find life. He told us His Words are spirit and they are life (John 6:63) and that man shall not live by bread alone, but by every Word that proceeds out of the mouth of God. (Mat 4:4) Yes, now when we eat His Word, the bread of life, and remember to make His unleavened Words an integral part of our lives, we will discern that the chaos is blocked by the Good Shepherd, who gave His life for the sheep.

His Word is our only protection from the myriad of philosophies and theologies bombarding us every day. When we eat and digest His Word, it becomes a vital part of our being. The Shepherd's Words will live in us and through us, as our "food for thought", word and action, providing us with His protection from chaos.

John 6:33 For the bread of God is he which cometh down from heaven, and giveth life unto the world.

# Life
## Chay

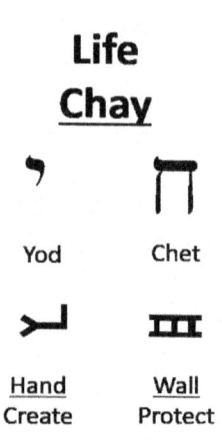

| י | ח |
|---|---|
| Yod | Chet |

| ⌐ | ☰ |
|---|---|
| <u>Hand</u> | <u>Wall</u> |
| Create | Protect |

## The Protecting Hand

Psalm 16:11 Thou wilt shew me the path of <u>life</u>: in thy presence is fulness of joy; at thy right hand there are pleasures for evermore.

The whole purpose of reality is to experience life. The creator's hand makes and sustains life, according to His purpose and His design. Revealed from the beginning, life was to be eternal and was only made possible by following his blueprint and plan. The tree of life was created to support our existence and survival throughout eternity. (Gen 3:22)

In the future, those that follow His design, His words and His commandments, will have access to the tree of life (Rev 22:14), because they will choose to follow his architecture, as revealed in His Word. Our existence is about living, and consciously spending time connecting with reality, experiencing harmony with the words of truth; the Spirit of life. (John 6:63)

He has come that we might have an abundant life (Jn 10:10) and through His grace we can understand His creation, His way, with His hand of protection within the laws that govern His design forever. (Titus 3:6) As in the past we are still to choose between life and death, blessings and curses, by obeying the voice of life (Deut 30:19-20) and cleaving to Him.

Yahshua (Jesus) is the light of the world (John 8:12) and we find life in Him, as He dispels the darkness and shows us the light of life. By following the light and living by it, we walk out of the darkness along the path He has established. He makes known to us the ways of life and in doing so, we become joyful in His presence. (Acts 2:28) A joyful life is the ultimate gift he came to give us now, and throughout eternity.

We are admonished to choose life in all that we do. Abundant life, as created and protected by Him, is realized the more we follow life His way, according to His design. Yes, the hand of the LORD, the creator, is the protecting hand of the universe. It is true and consistent with the words, "He has the whole world in His Hands".

2Peter 1:3 According as his divine power hath given unto us all things that pertain unto life and godliness, through the knowledge of him that hath called us to glory and virtue:

## Praise
## Halal

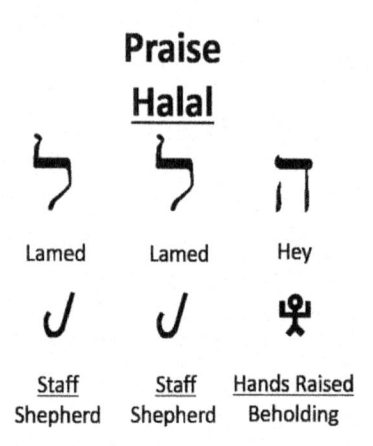

| ל | ל | ה |
|---|---|---|
| Lamed | Lamed | Hey |
| ␊ | ␊ | ☥ |
| <u>Staff</u> Shepherd | <u>Staff</u> Shepherd | <u>Hands Raised</u> Beholding |

## Behold The Shepherd of Shepherds

Psalm 117:1-2  O <u>praise</u> the LORD, all ye nations: praise him, all ye people. For his merciful kindness is great toward us: and the truth of the LORD endureth forever. <u>Praise</u> ye the LORD.

The very illustration of the Hebrew letters in the word, <u>Halal</u> (praise), shows our hands reaching up to the Shepherd of shepherds, seeking and beholding Him. The LORD of lords reveals Himself to us through His eternal creation. The universe makes Him known through the wonders of His Glory, established above the heavens and earth. (Ps 148)

We give thanks and praise to the LORD for all he has done and worship Him in joyful song and dance. We recognize Him as our King, because we are clothed with the beautiful and awesome gift of our salvation (Yahshua). (Ps 149)

Some have raised their hands in rage and frustration, for they have strayed from His ways, through lies and false teaching, making their knowledge foolish. Being backward, they raise their hands to God in madness, only recognizing Him through anger, not praise. (Isa 44:24-25)

By living in His Word, we praise His creation and make known His overwhelming grandeur and glory. We begin to understand his loving-kindness, judgment and righteousness in the earth and glory in the things that are His delight. (Jer 9:23-24) In doing this we bring praise and honor to His name.

In beholding the Shepherd of shepherds, we simultaneously reveal Him in our lives, while expressing our worship to Him. When reaching up to Him, acknowledging Him in our walk and seek to do His will. We make known to whom we are praising and giving fidelity. In doing this we present ourselves to Him as a living sacrifice, holy and acceptable to Him. (Rom 12:1-2)

Speak to and behold the Shepherd of shepherds. Seek His presence in your life. As you lift up your hands in praise to the LORD, you allow Him to live in you and through you.

Heb 13:15 By him therefore let us offer the sacrifice of praise to God continually, that is, the fruit of our lips giving thanks to his name.

# Fruit
## Pariy

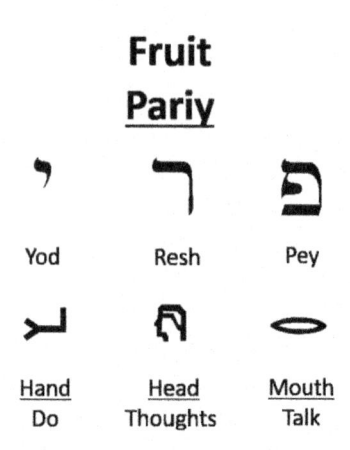

| Yod | Resh | Pey |
|---|---|---|
| Hand | Head | Mouth |
| Do | Thoughts | Talk |

## What is Said, Thought and Done

Proverbs 12:14  A man shall be satisfied with good by the fruit of his mouth: and the recompence of a man's hands shall be rendered unto him.

The Hebrew word for fruit is illustrated perfectly in the three letters pictured as a mouth, a head and a hand. Everything we do is initiated through our thoughts, and finds their way to what we say and what we do. The combination of thought word and action defines the essence of our being and communicates our identity to those around us.

Identifying the origin of our "seeds of thought" will help us decipher our words and actions. As we sow the seed of God's Word into our hearts, we will bear good fruit. (Luke 8:11-15; Mat 13:18-23)

The seed, the Word of God, planted in our hearts, germinates all that we think, say and do. (1 Peter 1:23)  The fruit of every tree is determined by the kind of seed planted.  As we journey through life, we find that the fruit of our thoughts, words and actions, impact every facet of our lives.  In our walk, we need to compare our ideas, terminology, and accomplishments, to the wisdom of the scriptures.

We should seek to understand and trust in His Word to carry out thoughts about life, as defined by His reality, knowing that He is a merciful discerner of the thoughts and intentions of our heart. (Isa 55:6-11) (Hebrews 4:12)

The seed, root and tree are brought to their fullness in the Messiah's words, "wherefore by their fruits you shall know them". (Mat 7:20) When living in the Spirit, we produce the fruit of goodness, righteousness and truth and we seek to understand what is acceptable to the Lord. We avoid the unfruitful works of darkness and speak out against it, because we have God's Word dwelling in our thoughts.  (Eph 5:9-11).

As we walk in the Spirit, we germinate the seed and fruit of the Spirit in our hearts, impacting all that we say, think and do.  (Gal 5:22-25)

John 15:5   I am the vine, ye are the branches: He that abideth in me, and I in Him, the same bringeth forth much fruit: for without me ye can do nothing.

# Understanding
## Biyn

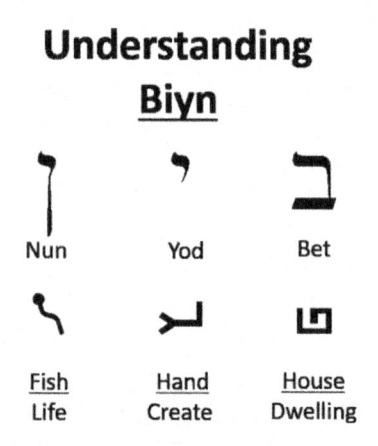

| Nun | Yod | Bet |
|---|---|---|
| Fish | Hand | House |
| Life | Create | Dwelling |

## The House Created for Life

Ps 119:130  The entrance of thy words giveth light; it giveth <u>understanding</u> unto the simple.

Everything the LORD does is for one overall purpose, and that is to nurture life. His whole design for the reality He created is all about life. His long term ambition is to show us that the "House" He created for us to live in can only survive in perpetuity by applying the principles that are in harmony with His Words. When we seek His Words in all things, our minds are enlightened and we can begin to understand life from His eternal perspective.

He will direct our paths, when we trust Him in all our ways and consult Him for our understanding. (Prov 3:5-6) One's understanding is darkened by ignorance, when alienated from the life the LORD has designed. (Eph 4:18) Only with the light of His Word hid in our heart, discover the truths that support life philosophies that oppose His creat 119:11)

His ways are life; sin is entropy, and s     .s in death. (Rom 6:23) It is very clear; the LORD's Words bring life and sin is an approach to life that is equated to and creates entropy leading to death. Understanding sees the House created for life and does what can be done to promote the creators agenda of life.

We can certainly see the chaos in the world today operating out of harmony with His understanding of "being" and His original design. The "House" fashioned for life is not a marginal existence; rather an abundant life is the LORD's agenda. (John 10:10) When we study His Word and seek to live in accord with His ways, we develop the understanding that He wants us to have, as the basis for engaging ourselves, other people and all facets of His creation.

When we apply His understanding, we truly find wisdom, and we know that living in His "House" we find the way, the truth and the life, as He created it and desired it to be for us.

Col 1:9 For this cause we also, since the day we heard it, do not cease to pray for you, and to desire that ye may be filled with the knowledge of his will in all wisdom and spiritual understanding.

**Eye**
**Ayin**

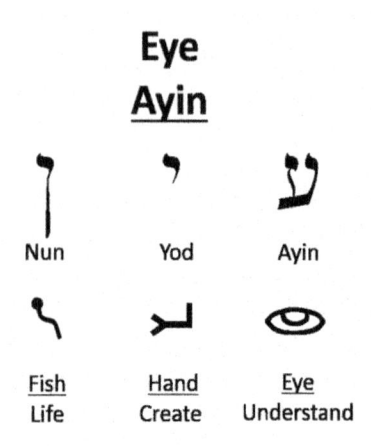

| Nun | Yod | Ayin |
|---|---|---|

| Fish | Hand | Eye |
|---|---|---|
| Life | Create | Understand |

## See/Understand The Hand of Life

Jeremiah 5:21  Hear now this, O foolish people, and without understanding; which have <u>eyes</u>, and see not; which have ears, and hear not:

When we open our eyes of understanding we see God's whole focus is on life.  The more we understand the LORD, the more we see His heart in the purpose and reason for life, is all about seeing life, His way!  When we truly see, we understand His hand creating, establishing, defining and supporting life.  Unlike the enemy that promotes death and anything that produces and supports chaos, our Creator's hand is all about life.  Two totally opposed objectives come into our vision and understanding; life vs. death.

Yahshua (Jesus) said, He came that we might have life and have it more abundantly. (John 10:10)  Not only do we have the promise of eternal life, but also, we have the opportunity to experience life now. Being filled by His Word, which is the Spirit of life, we can now see and know what enhances and supports life; His Way!

What is it all about? Living ….. experiencing reality each moment. Reality: our sight, smell, touch, taste, hearing and our being; all facets of our connection with life, the Temple of the Holy Spirit, where He lives within us.   (1 Cor 3:16)

Life is not an accident to be diminished, but a gift to be cherished, respected and protected. The Creator established life as His primary focus and purpose in the universe. The whole heart of salvation is life. Those who see this very same reality choose life, uphold His Word, and realize the associated blessings that come with it. (Rom 6:22-23)

When we really know, truth is what we see, and truly see what we know and understand, The Spirit of Life is observed! His Reality …His Truth. (John 6:63) He wants us to be enlightened about His creation, a creation that was established to be enjoyed forever and ever. When we see His hand and the intended plan for life, we begin to understand why He died to give us the blessed hope and inheritance, eternal life.

Eph 1:18 The eyes of your understanding being enlightened; that ye may know what is the hope of his calling, and what the riches of the glory of His inheritance in the saints,

## Presence / Face
## Panayim

| Mem | Yod | Nun | Pey |
|---|---|---|---|
| Water | Hand | Fish | Mouth |
| Chaos | Hold | Life | Voice |

### The Voice of Life with Hold on the Chaos

Ps 16:11  Thou wilt shew me the path of life: in thy presence is fullness of joy; at thy right hand there are pleasures for evermore.

A joyous life is one filled with life, without chaos. The LORD's face shinning upon us is a true blessing (Num 6:23-27), when we hear His voice of life and understand that the purpose of His hand is to suppress the chaos around us.

He came that we would have an abundant life, one without destruction and death. (John 10:10) The more we can understand His Word, the voice of life, meditate on it, and put it into practice, the more we will realize the objective of His design and His presence with us.

As we trust in His ways, pray and seek His face, we recognize that He will not forsake us and He will protect us in the secret of His presence. (Psalm 27:8; Psalm 31:19-20) We also experience more of God's liberation in our lives, as we pursue his face, look to Him in all things and see His Spirit at work. By beholding Him we become changed, we practice His presence in our day to day experience, and are transformed to His original design. (2Cor 3:17-18)

We can enhance His companionship in our lives by avoiding chaos and seeking those things that promote life. For when we think and do what is true, honest, just, pure, lovely, reputable, excellent, and praiseworthy, we invite His presence and His peace to be with us. (Phil 4:8-9) We witness the destruction of the authority connected to chaos by living in the presence of God. We invite the LORD's countenance upon us, realizing peace and gladness. (Psalm 4:6-8)

In everything we should seek all things that promote life and avoid everything and anything that enhances chaos. As we witness the things of this world, we can identify those things that he would smile upon and the things He would frown upon. His presence is linked with whatever advances life and purges chaos (sin). Upon conversion, living in His presence, we hear the voice of life and see the removal of the chaos.

Acts 3:19 Repent ye therefore, and be converted, that your sins be blotted out, when the time of refreshing shall come from the presence of the Lord;

# Wisdom
## Chokmah

| ה | מ | כ | ח |
|---|---|---|---|
| Hey | Mem | Kaf | Chet |
| Hands Raised | Water | Palm | Wall |
| Revealed | Chaos | Bless | Protect |

## Protect the Blessing, Chaos Revealed

Prov 4:5-7   Get wisdom, get understanding: forget it not; neither decline from the words of my mouth.  Forsake her not, and she shall preserve thee: love her, and she shall keep thee.  Wisdom is the principal thing; therefore get wisdom: and with all thy getting get understanding.

True wisdom is from the LORD and always looks to protect the blessings of life, while exposing the chaos for what it is….decay.  Knowledge and intelligence is of value, only when it is used for enhancing life and eliminating disorder.  Improving ones knowledge is important and can be used for good, as long as it strengthens and blesses the lives around us.  Wisdom is the application of knowledge.  Wisdom is not about how smart you are, but how you are smart!  The how of being smart is where wisdom enters.  Wisdom is life enhanced and chaos uncovered.

Throughout the scriptures, and numerous times in the Proverbs, wisdom is proclaimed to be essential for life; however fools reject and despise God's wisdom. (Prov 1:2-7)

Many choices are put before us today, prior to entering the land of promise. We also are to apply wisdom, choosing life with blessing, instead of death with curses and chaos. (Deut 30:19-20) When we study God's word and apply His instructions, we find our understanding enhanced, as we see the benefits of life improved around us. Wisdom is a function of protecting and following the Creator's instruction manual. (Deut 4:6)

It does not take a Ph.D. or Th.D. to understand what wisdom is or what is wisdom. Simply by following His Words on His Path, His Way, we will walk in the wisdom that is from above. Our Creator has proven true understanding, as any concept that supports His beautiful gift of life. Wisdom identifies where life is compromised and where life can be enriched by knowing His Word.

God's wisdom is fully discovered when seen in action. We find genuine wisdom, as defined by the LORD, when blessings are protected and chaos is revealed through applying His Word.

James 3:17 But the wisdom that is from above is first pure, then peaceable, gentle, and easy to be intreated, full of mercy and good fruits, without partiality and without hypocrisy.

## Voice
## Qowl

| ל | ו | ק |
|---|---|---|
| Lamed | Vav | Kof |
| ✓ | Y | ᛩ |
| Staff | Nail | Back of Head |
| Shepherd | Connect | Follow |

## Follow and Connect to The Shepherd

Jeremiah 7:23   But this thing commanded I them, saying Obey my voice, and I will be your God, and ye shall be my people: and walk ye in all the ways that I have commanded you, that it may be well unto you.

We recognize our Shepherd's voice and follow what is connected to and supported by His Word. THE voice is identified by the truth, revealed within the communication to us. No one can counterfeit His voice, for His voice is the voice of reality/truth. Whether He speaks in a still small voice, in thunder or through His people, the message is consistent: salvation, sanctification, and the restoration of life.

Everyone hears voices. Who is speaking? Listen for The voice to be in harmony with Him. He wants us to follow His Words, for they are the voice of life, and all of His communication to us will support the essence and purpose of our being. When we study His Word, we can differentiate between the many voices we hear and verify that the voice we are following is His. Our Shepherd would never ask us to do anything that is not in harmony with the Words of Scripture. By eating His Word, the Bread of Life, we become more aware of His utterance, the Voice of Life, that is within us and guiding us.

When we recognize His voice and follow Him now, we will also hear His voice calling us, upon the Shepherd's return to this earth, even though we may be in the grave. (John 5:25)   The Shepherd of our lives is then forever revealed. The Lord said, everyone that is of the truth hears His voice. (John 18:37)

When we obey His voice now, we reveal who we are following. We make known the identity of our Shepherd.  Since we listen for and follow what is connected to His voice wherever we go, we are the sheep of His pasture. (Ps 79:13; 100:3; 95:7-8)

Everyone is following, believing in, adhering to, and/or basing their lives on a given worldview. We need to make sure we know who the authority of that worldview is we are following. We hear our Shepherd; He knows us; we follow.

John 10:27   My sheep hear my voice, and I know them, and they follow me.

# Fear / Afraid
## Yare'

| א | ר | י |
|---|---|---|
| Aleph | Resh | Yod |
| ⌐ See 𐤓 | | ⌐ |
| Head's Strength | | |
| Ox | Head | Hand |
| Strength | Man | Create |

## The Hand You See

Psalm 34:7-9   The angel of the LORD encampeth round about them that <u>fear</u> him, and delivereth them.  O taste and see that the LORD is good:  blessed is the man that trusteth in him.  O <u>fear</u> the LORD, ye his saints: for there is no want to them that <u>fear</u> him.

Fear is trusting God's hand in all things; the hand that we see.  Sometimes it is difficult to reconcile the fear of God with love, until we put our trust completely into the hand of God and try to perceive things from His frame of reference.  As we grow in Him, we will see the "hand of the LORD" in what was, is now, and will be.

Through His Word we begin to discern things from His comprehensive, eternal perspective.  (Josh 4:23-24)  In the middle of anguish from our foes, we will have confidence in His hand of protection, because the LORD is the strength of our lives. With Him in our lives, what is there to be afraid of? (Ps 27:1-3) The LORD has given us a spirit of power, love, and a sound mind, not a spirit of fear. (2Tim 1:7)

In the midst of the world's chaos, sometimes it is hard to see His hand and purpose, while in the "center of the storm". Many times we do not know the reason or comprehend the situation we are experiencing, until the storm is over, the clouds clear, and we see the light again. We now begin to perceive His plan unfold and we understand our part in His tapestry. We need to trust Him, as all things are in His Hands. We will see His hand weaving His pattern into all things, even in the valleys of life. (Gen 50:20; Ps 23:4)

As we journey within His creation and destiny to the Land of Promise, the LORD wants us to walk in His ways, love Him, serve Him, and see His hand in the midst of our fears.   (Deut 10:11-14)

We can reconcile all of the texts of scripture relating to fear by seeing the original meaning of the letters and pictures that form the Hebrew word Yare'. Fear is seeing His hand in all things, as The Hand we see working, and realizing that all things work together for good to those who love God and are the called according to His purpose. (Rom 8:28)

Eph 5:21  Submitting yourselves one to another in the fear of God.

**Walk**

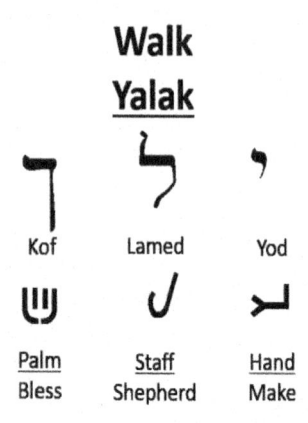

**Yalak**

| Kof | Lamed | Yod |
|---|---|---|
| Palm | Staff | Hand |
| Bless | Shepherd | Make |

## The Hand of The Shepherd's Blessing

Ps 23:4   Yea, though I walk through the valley of the shadow of death, I will fear no evil: for thou art with me; thy rod and thy staff they comfort me.

Take His hand and walk with Him, leading you into the blessings of life.  We take His hand, because we want to go with the Shepherd and the Shepherd to go with us.  It is the LORD's desire that we walk with Him, Hand in hand, following His way, comforted by His rod and staff.  (Ps 143:8)

Solely, with His hand guiding us and directing us, can we walk on the path He has prepared for us.  Only in holding His hand can we walk in truth and experience the reality He has established.  As a parent nurtures and directs the lives of their children, so our Shepherd walks with us as our teacher, and counselor in every aspect of our daily lives. His Words of wisdom lead us though our daily lives each day, as we take hold of His Words of guidance and blessing.

As we experience life each day, we need to look to Him, and walk as He walked, for He is our example, (1John 2:6) and we know that there is no condemnation walking with Him in the Spirit. (Rom 8:1) He will instruct us and lead us in the way we should go. He will dwell in us and walk in and with us. (Ps 32:8; 2Cor 6:16) As we walk in the light that He provides on the pathway of life (1John 1:7), we find life the way He designed it, and we can be assured that He is with us everywhere we go. (Joshua 1:9) When walking with Him, we will not live in darkness, as He is the light of life, showing us the path. (John 8:12)

The invitation stands, to come and walk with Him through the valleys and mountain tops of life, holding tight to His hand, yielding in obedience, dying to self in Him, with complete confidence in His Words. He teaches us how to walk with Him in newness of life, where life's blessings are actually found. (Rom 6:4-10)

Cling to the hand of our Shepherd and walk with His blessing, in the love He has created for us.

2 John 1:6 And this is love, that we walk after his commandments. This is the commandment, That, as ye have heard from the beginning, ye should walk in it.

# Way
## Derek

| Kof | Resh | Dalet |
|---|---|---|
| Palm / Bless | Head / Man | Door / Entrance |

## The Door to Man's Blessing

Prov 8:32-35   Now therefore hearken unto me, O ye children: for blessed are they that keep my ways.  Hear instruction, and be wise, and refuse it not.  Blessed is the man that heareth me, watching daily at my gates, waiting at the posts of my doors.  For whoso findeth me findeth life, and shall obtain favor of the LORD.

Our path is determined by walking in the way you have set before us.  LORD we come to you through the door into our Father's house to find blessing.  In seeking to understand your words, do we find life, the way you designed it.  In your Word we find the wisdom to make our daily decisions.  You have set before us life and death, blessings and curses.  (Deut 30:19-20)  In choosing your ways we find life and blessing.  While choosing to live in covenant with you, the Good Shepherd, we listen for your voice to show us the way of life now and forever. (John 10:27-28)

While on the path of life and on the many roads travelled, we use a map and follow the signs along the way to our destination. The key is to study and know the map, avoid the detours and continue to consult Him, the Mapmaker, as our guide when taking each step along the journey. In consultation with our Surveyor, we walk in the Spirit on the path he has established.

As the Creator, the LORD has defined life through His straight gate and told us the way is narrow. (Mat 7:14) Let us enter His gateway and find life, the way He intended it to be. It is not about what is "cool", who is doing it, or that "everybody does it". It is about finding His way to live, the life he designed for us to experience. All other ways are subject to creating chaos and destruction in life. His way, found in His Word, provides the avenue for us to experience His truth. It is the only reality that is not vain, hopeless, unproductive or destructive, but is forever producing life for our delight. (Ps 119:37)

He is the entry door to the way, the truth and the life, where we find the Father waiting to bless us on our journey, along the way though the curves, dead ends, mountain tops and valleys of life.

John 14:6 Jesus saith unto him, I am the way, the truth, and the life: no man cometh unto the Father, but by me.

# Know
## Yada

| Ayin | Dalet | Yod |
|------|-------|-----|
| Eye  | Door  | Hand |
| Understand | Entrance | Create |

## The Hand at The Door is Understood

Psalm 143:8   Cause me to hear thy loving-kindness in the morning; for in thee do I trust: cause me to <u>know</u> the way wherein I should walk; for I lift up my soul unto thee.

When we hear the Hand that knocks and choose to allow entry through the door into our lives, into our minds and hearts, we come to know and experience who is at the front door of our house. Knowing is then fully experienced when we live out and apply the principles we nurture to comprehend.

When understanding our faith, we do what we believe, realizing that our faith goes beyond an intellectual comprehension, but a living faith that appreciates and applies it to life.  As it is said, faith without works is dead.  (James 2:17) Faith and understanding becomes knowing what we believe when applied. As we continue to apply the scriptures to our lives, we know the voice at the door, trust in His ways, and invite Him in to live in us and fellowship with us. (Rev 3:20)

Beyond understanding, do you know what you understand, or understand what you know? As we study the scriptures and practice the truths of life, we find the entrance to understanding and we grow to know His ways more deeply. (Ps 25:4-5) As we unite with His instruction and identify with the realities of life, we come to know, that we really know, the hand that is nurturing us is the Creator of all things.

Really knowing is experiencing, applying, validating, and testing God's Word in the context of our lives and the world around us. We can truly see the reality of the knowledge, wisdom and beauty of His revelation. Only then can we discern who is looking to enter the door of our lives. The more we understand about who is at the door of our hearts, our house, the more we can confirm, if the Hand at the door is the Creator, the LORD of eternal life. (1John 5:20)

Ephesians 1:17-18  That the God of our Lord Jesus Christ, the Father of glory, may give unto you the spirit of wisdom and revelation in the knowledge of him: the eyes of your understanding being enlightened; that ye may know what is the hope of his calling, and what the riches of the glory of his inheritance in the saints.

## Profane
## Chalal

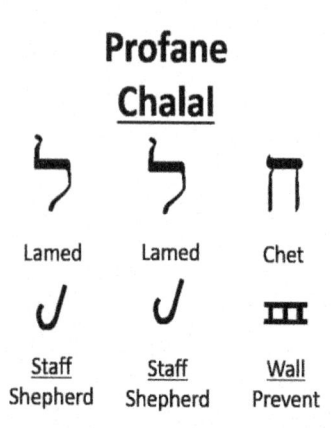

| Lamed | Lamed | Chet |
|---|---|---|
| Staff | Staff | Wall |
| Shepherd | Shepherd | Prevent |

## Prevent The Shepherd of Shepherd's

Ez 36:23  And I will sanctify my great name, which was profaned among the heathen, which ye have profaned in the midst of them; and the heathen shall know that I am the LORD, saith the Lord GOD, when I shall be sanctified in you before their eyes.

When we study and apply the "Word of Truth" to our lives, we bring glory to the LORD. We are admonished to avoid discussions that block the LORD from our being, as this profanity leads to ungodliness. Anything that prevents us from listening and following His covenant is against Him and leads to defilement. Everything that prevents His Word in our lives is "Chalal", thwarting Him from living in and through us.

In prayer (Palal), we speak to the Shepherd of shepherd's. In praise (Halal), we behold the

Shepherd of shepherd's. When one profanes, one blocks the Shepherd of shepherd's from their thoughts, words and actions. The good news is, that even though one may block Him, by not glorifying Him or rejecting Him in our walk, He is ever there to forgive us when we seek Him in a prayer of confession. (1 John 1:7-9)

Open your heart to Him and walk with Him in the Spirit. Do not avoid the Spirit, fulfilling the lusts of the flesh, which blocks Him from our lives, but pursue the Spirit and live in the fruit of love, joy, peace, patience, gentleness, goodness, faith, meekness, and temperance in all things. (Gal 5:16-25) Blocking the Shepherd of shepherd's defiles the temple of God and prevents Him from living in us. (1Cor 3:16-17) Seek His presence and be open to reside in and with Him, guided by His Spirit.

The LORD wants us to be in an attitude of prayer and to praise Him, as we live our lives from hour to hour in His presence. Blocking Him from communing with us in our lives, not only does harm to us, but also, to those around us. We experience more clearly what He envisioned, when we do not block the Shepherd of Shepherd's from our lives and others.

2 Tim 2:15-16 Study to shew thyself approved unto God, a workman that needeth not to be ashamed, rightly dividing the word of truth. But shun profane and vane babblings: for they will increase unto more ungodliness.

# Sin
## Chata'

| א | ט | ח |
|---|---|---|
| Aleph | Tet | Chet |

| 𐤀 | ⊗ | ⊟ |
|---|---|---|
| <u>Ox</u> | <u>Basket</u> | <u>Wall</u> |
| Strength | Surround | Prevent |

## Prevent and Surround your Strength

Psalm 119:11   Thy word have I hid in mine heart, that I might not <u>sin</u> against thee.

Sin is simply anything we do that is out of harmony with God's word. Everything we do not in accord with Him prevents and limits our strength to live the life He conceived. The laws He has established govern all aspects of our lives, not as limitations, as some proclaim, but as the way to experience the realities of an abundant life, as He fashioned it. (John 10:10)

The wages of sin is death, not life. (Rom 6:23) Sin prevents and limits our ability to experience His vision and purpose for our lives. By not following His recipe, we block out the very ingredients needed to produce His ultimate and desired outcome, life now and forever. He wants us to feast and have all the nutrition life awards.

The more we trust in His word, we realize that His commandments are for our benefit and are not against us. The good news of the Gospel informs us that our sins are forgiven and that the blood of Yahshua (Jesus) also cleanses us from sin, as we walk in the Spirit, in the light of His Word. (1John 1:5-10; Rom 8:4-10) His Words are Spirit and life; His Word is a lamp unto our feet and a light unto our path; His instructions are the way of life. (John 6:63; Ps 119:105; Prov 6:23)

The scriptures admonish us to behold the "lamb of God" who takes away the sin of the world. When we understand, believe and grow in the good news of salvation, we separate ourselves from what the LORD defines as sin. His design of reality points out the dichotomy of opposites in terms of light and dark, up and down, blessings and curses, life and death, His Way and the way of sin, etc. Sin exists as a contrast to life, demonstrating the entropy that He wants us to avoid, and life, as the reality He wants for us.

When we receive Him, He gives us power to become the sons of God. (John 1:12-13) Our strength will be renewed, not blocked or limited, and we will experience life more fully, when done His Way, according to His sinless design.

1 John 2:1 My little children, these things write I unto you, that ye sin not. And if any man sin, we have an advocate with the Father, Jesus Christ the righteous:

# Forgive / Pardon
## Salach

| ח | ל | ס |
|---|---|---|
| Chet | Lamed | Samech |
| Wall | Staff | Prop |
| Protect | Shepherd | Support |

## Supported by The Shepherd's Protection

2 Chron 7:14   If my people, which are called by my name, shall humble themselves, and pray, and seek my face, and turn from their wicked ways; then I will hear from heaven, and will forgive their sin, and will heal their land.

We are supported by the Shepherd's protection every time we seek His face and pray for forgiveness. His promise is that He will forgive us and cleanse us from all unrighteous behavior. Through grace, now being forgiven from sin and not under the penalty of law, He wants us to be servants of righteousness and to follow Him in our daily walk. (Rom 6:15 -18)

Forgiveness works both ways; for as we depend on Him for pardon, we also depend on Him for His guidance in the decisions we make each moment.  His forgiveness assists us each day, while we live in the Spirit forgiving others in our daily walk, realizing that He also forgives us in our imperfections. (Luke 11:4)

While walking with Him in the Spirit of forgiveness, we are very conscious of our need to grow in His Word, and to leave our sins behind us. In so doing, we individually and collectively will find healing in our lives. The healing will spread across the land and peace will come to the world. Only He has the power to forgive us. He will cover us from the wages of sin and shield us from the $2^{nd}$ death, because we can depend on the Good Shepherd's protection. (Rom 6:23)

Forgiveness is a gift of grace and assists us in the process of sanctification, whereby we mortify the deeds of the flesh and seek His face in all things, because we are led by His Spirit. (Rom 8:13 -15) As we grow in grace and realize the gift of forgiveness, we want to follow His ways. Forgiveness through His grace is not a license to ignore His words of life, but a motivator to apply His beautiful instructions as the only way to live.

In the renewed Covenant, His law is written on our hearts; our iniquity is forgiven and not remembered. This is our Shepherd's pardon and promise of protection for life. (Jer 31:31-34)

1 John 1:9  If we confess our sins, he is faithful and just to forgive us our sins, and to cleanse us from all unrighteousness.

# Hope / Expectation
## Tiqvah

| ה | ו | ק | ת |
|---|---|---|---|
| Hey | Vav | Kof | Tav |
| Hands Raised | Nail | Back of Head | Cross |
| Revealed | Connect | Follow | Covenant |

## Covenant Following the Nail Revealed

Psalm 71:5  For thou art my hope, O Lord GOD: thou art my trust from my youth.

Revealed in the only sign to be given, was the sign of the prophet Jonah, life after three days and nights in the belly of the whale. (Mat 12:39-40) Prophetically, THE sign followed the crucifixion nail, hope was revealed to us through the resurrection after 3 days and nights. The hope of eternal life was given through His grace. (Titus 3:7; 2 Thes 2:16-17)

Hope refers to an attachment to something not yet fully made manifest and yet is connected to what is made known. We wait patiently for the glorious return of Yahshua. (Jesus) (Titus 2:13) Hope is not a wish, but an expectation of a secure promise to be practiced by those who are grounded in faith and experience comfort in the

Holy Scriptures. (Col 1:21-23; Rom.

As we read His Word and understand
of life found in His inheritance, we disc
hope of His calling, and we trust in Him
our lives. (Eph 1:18-19; 1 Pet 1:3-5; Prov 3:5-6)
The very heart of our faith, substantiating that
our confidence is not in vain, is seen in the
crucifixion and resurrection of Yahshua. We
would have no assurance in life, if Yahshua did
not rise from the dead and our faith would be in
vain. (1 Cor 15:14)

The Lord's resurrection provides us with a
perspective that allows us to go beyond the
artificial expectations and confidence in
mankind, to a hope that gives us peace and joy,
for it is written and validated by God Himself.

It is awesome to recognize that before the
foundation of the world, the focal point of our
faith was illustrated in the very word that we rest
upon. Hope: where we put our trust. The
covenant that follows the nail was revealed to
us! Now we may experience THE blessed hope
and realize the covenant in our lives.

I Peter 1:19-21  But the precious blood of Christ,
as a lamb without blemish and without spot: who
verily was foreordained before the foundation of
the world, but was manifest in these last times
for you, Who by him do believe in God, that
raised him up from the dead, and gave him
glory; that your faith and hope might be in God.

# Truth
## Emeth

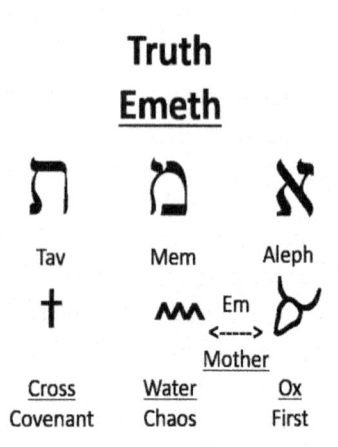

| ת | מ | א |
|---|---|---|
| Tav | Mem | Aleph |
| † | ᴧᴧ | Ƅ |
| | Em <-----> Mother | |
| Cross | Water | Ox |
| Covenant | Chaos | First |

## Mother of The Covenant

Psalm 25:5 Lead me in thy truth, and teach me: for thou art the God of my salvation; on thee do I wait all the day.

Mother, the bond of the family, provides us with a perfect picture of the one who gives birth to the covenant, where truth is nurtured and protected. In the covenant we find the truth of life is based on its agreement and consistency with reality. Only in and through His word do we find, connect with, and validate reality. His true story is found in HIStory, where his laws are confirmed by the blessings and curses witnessed in society. When not following truth, day to day life cannot sustain itself and eventually implodes within the chaos.

The LORD told us that when we continue in His Word we are His disciples and set free, because we will know the truth. (John 8:31-32) In His word we find the purpose and reality of our existence in this world. When we know His Word and understand what is relevant to life, we find that we can be set free from the many encumbrances an alternate reality imposes on us. Desiring truth asserts wisdom, a reality that upholds life and denounces chaos. (Psalm 51:6)

A mother gives birth to life, protects, nurtures, only wants the best that life has to give, and is the same idea portrayed in the word truth. Life cannot be authentic without truth. Truth is essential for a prolonged meaningful existence.

The foundation and principle of truth is about having a valid perspective regarding reality and authenticity. Our faith cannot be substantiated or depended upon, if it is not based on truth and facts about our being. Life cannot be lived out in a fantasy world without the evolution of chaos.

It is a beautiful picture for us to realize that truth is embodied in a mother. She gives birth to the symbol of the covenant, the sign of our faith, and basis for life. Truth can be found in the spirit of revealing a sanctified life. (John17:17) Giving birth is a requirement fundamental to our existence and so is knowing His Word, THE truth about life, the mother of the covenant.

John 14:6 Jesus saith unto him, I am the way, the truth, and the life: no man cometh unto the father, but by me.

# Love
## Ahab

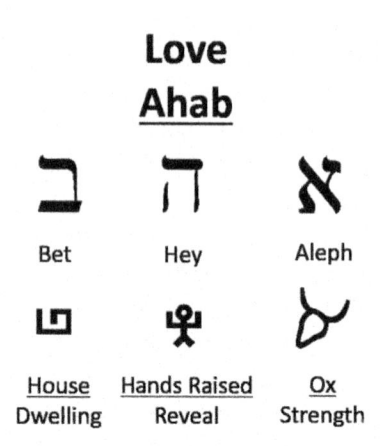

| ב | ה | א |
|---|---|---|
| Bet | Hey | Aleph |
| House | Hands Raised | Ox |
| Dwelling | Reveal | Strength |

## Strength Revealed in The House

Deut 6:5   And thou shalt <u>love</u> the LORD thy God with all thine heart, and with all thy soul, and with all thy might.

Added into the heart of the two letter word Father, is the letter Hey. (see page 35)  This depicts "Beholding the Father", the word Ahab/Love, illustrates the perfect picture of Love. He wants us to behold Him as the ideal example and meaning of true, complete love.  The designer of the universe established love to be the most important factor representing the reality He created.

The overall law of creation is based on love. That is why out of love for us, He gave His Son to die in our place, so we would have life in eternity.  Love is the essential ingredient for life to be sustained on this planet.  Anything short of love will eventually generate chaos, which is currently visible in the various forms of death and destruction existing in the world today.

His most important fundamental instruction to us is to love; to love Him first and foremost, then to love our neighbor as ourselves. (Deut 6:5; Lev 19:18; Mark 12:29-31) In beholding Him at the outset, we understand our value. God Himself died to prove and validate His love for us! Only then can we love others, for the reason that we need to comprehend our importance and significance to Him first. We are to love ourselves in this context, because He values us. Yes, after falling in love with God, you must first love yourself, before you can love others.

The identification of God being love, perfectly describes Him and His character, because God is Love! (1 John 4:16-21) We need to be conscious of His design and live in the context of love. Living in His context of love is vital and critical for our universe to thrive and survive. When we believe in the love that He first had toward us, we dwell in Him, He takes residence in us, and we can love others more completely. Yes, love, the power and strength revealed in His house, is found in beholding Him, our Father in heaven, who so loved the world.

John 3:16 For God so loved the world, that he gave his only begotten Son, that whosoever believeth in Him should not perish, but have everlasting life.

# Joy / Rejoice / Sing
## Ranan

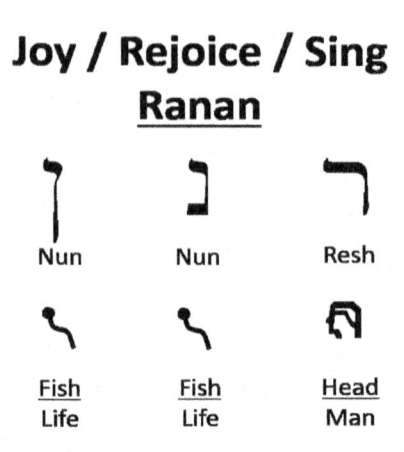

| Nun | Nun | Resh |
|---|---|---|
| Fish Life | Fish Life | Head Man |

## Man with The Life of Life

Ps 5:11   But let all those who put their trust in thee rejoice: let them ever shout for joy, because thou defendest them: let them also that love thy name be joyful in thee.

Joy is realized when we celebrate life. As we eat more of the bread of life, we grow in the Spirit and knowledge of Him. Our appreciation for life, and all that supports life, becomes our focus and desire, resulting in singing, rejoicing and celebration.

It is all about life. About our life now and life eternal, promised by our Father.  (John 3:16; 10:10)   Internalizing and trusting our faith in Him brings about a joy for life and a song in our hearts.  (Ps 28:7)

The words that He speaks to us brings joy in

living the "life of life". Our joy becomes even fuller, the more we live out His words. He told us His words are Spirit and life and that He is the bread of life. Our hearts sing and rejoice louder and louder, the more we realize His saving grace and practice His design for living.

The Scriptures were written to make known the LORD to us, and throughout the revealing, that our joy may be full. (1 John 1:4) He endured the most brutal death to deliver us and to give us the joy of life. We sing about the gift of His deliverance, salvation and righteousness. (Heb 12:2; Ps 51:14-15) Yes, when we understand the house He created for life, we resonate with joyful praise in our being. Let us make a joyful noise to the Rock of our salvation and let us come into His presence with thanksgiving. (Ps 95:1-3) Recognizing what He has done for us, we come into a deeper relationship with Him.

When our thoughts contemplate the awesomeness of His creation, and we begin to recognize the ultimate plan He has for His people, we get a glimpse into the joy He intended for us. His will for us will be done, on earth, as it is in heaven. (Mat 6:10) Seek His face in our lives, and in His presence we find the joy He envisioned, the "life of life", with Him, in Him and from Him; a joy money cannot buy.

John 15:11 These things have I spoken unto you, that my joy may remain in you, and that your joy might be full.

# Redeem
## Padah

| ה | ד | פ |
|---|---|---|
| Hey | Dalet | Pey |

| Hands Raised | Door | Mouth |
|---|---|---|
| Reveal | Entrance | Voice |

## The Voice of The Door Revealed

Ps 34:22; 71:23 The LORD redeemeth the soul of his servants: and none of them that trust in him shall be desolate. My lips shall greatly rejoice when I sing unto thee; and my soul, which thou hast redeemed.

Yahshua (Jesus) is the Door. We enter the Father's House through Him and through His voice we find redemption. He has told us that through His Blood and Words we have eternal life. When we search the Scriptures, we find they testify of Yahshua and He is the One, through His voice, that will give us life, a life more abundant. His voice is the voice that we should be listening for and following in our daily walk, as we are confronted with many voices. What are these voices representing? Who's message are they presenting? Only the voice consistent with Scripture will provide us with the redemption, rescue and freedom that He has planned for us.

Adam and Eve were familiar with God's voice in the garden and were sidetracked when they followed another voice, a voice that contradicted God's Word. God has demonstrated, that in His voice we find blessing, and when not pursuing His Words, we will find trouble and chaos. Yahshua is also the Door to the sheepfold, and He is the Shepherd of the sheep. (John 10:9) It is His voice that calls us into the sheepfold, into fellowship with Him. He has told us that His sheep hear His voice. Listen for His voice and follow Him as he calls you and do not listen to any stranger's voice, but flee from the stranger.

"I stand at the door and knock. If any man hears my voice, I will come into him and feast with him and he with me." (Rev 3:20) Establish Him as the Door to your life and only allow entry to your heart when you hear the Words He speaks, for they are spirit and life. (John 6:63)

He is both the voice of the door to His house and the voice at the door of our hearts. Keep His Words in your heart and He will dwell in you and you will dwell in Him through the Spirit. (1John 3:24) The Voice at The Door Reveals our rescue and redemption now and in the world to come. Hear The Voice and enter The Door.

John 10:9 I am the Door: by me if any man enter in, he shall be saved, and shall go in and out, and find pasture.

## Salvation
## Yahshua

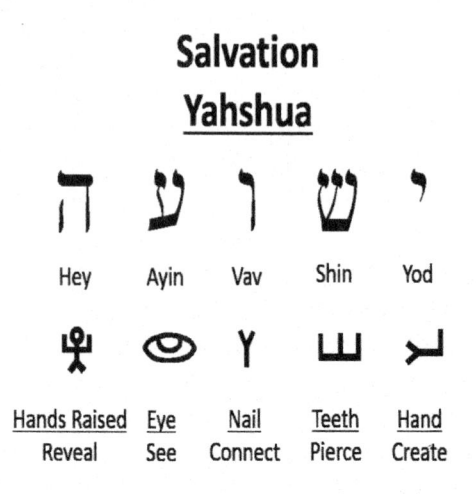

| ה | ע | ו | שׁ | י |
|---|---|---|---|---|
| Hey | Ayin | Vav | Shin | Yod |
| Hands Raised | Eye | Nail | Teeth | Hand |
| Reveal | See | Connect | Pierce | Create |

## Hand Pierced by the Nail Seen Revealed

Ps 62:2  He only is my rock and my <u>Salvation;</u> he is my defense; I should not be greatly moved.

The name Yahshua, transliterated to Jesus, the most common reference to the Messiah's name today, is a profound prophecy of His identity and mission on this earth.  As you can see, the letters within His name actually describe His crucifixion, thousands of years before the Romans used this type of torture for capital punishment.

Referring to the Messiah, Isaiah said that He was pierced through for our transgressions; He was crushed for our iniquities; the chastening of our well being fell upon Him.  And by His scourging we are healed.  (Isaiah 53:5)
The events of Isaiah 53 and the letters of

Yahshua's name clearly describe how and in Whom our salvation is found. It is not a coincidence that the very name of the One who came into this world to rescue and provide us with the very essence of His purpose, illustrates the exact description of His sacrificial death.

It is only God Himself who could rescue and deliver us from the penalty of sin. We trust in His mercy and rejoice in His salvation. (Ps 13:5) He reveals Himself within His Name and we behold the gift of His life and death for our redemption and liberation.

The prophetic nature of the Messiah's Name, Salvation, provides us His identification, being the only valid sacrifice for our sins and rescue from chaos on this planet. The phenomenon of His real Name, through translations and transliterations, unfortunately has been lost over time. The divine inspiration of Scripture is discovered again in a profound way, when one realizes the foretelling of His life and death has been in front of us from the beginning.

His hands were pierced to fulfill the nature of His death to us, as the Savior at His first coming. Yet again "in that day", he will be seen, when he returns to reveal Himself at His second coming. (Zech 12:9-10)

Acts 4:12 Niether is there salvation in any other: for there is none other name under heaven given among men, whereby we must be saved.

# Foolish / Fool / Stupid
## Nabal

| ל | ב | נ |
|---|---|---|
| Lamed | Bet | Nun |

| Staff | House | Fish |
|---|---|---|
| Shepherd | Dwelling | Life |

## Life outside The House of The Shepherd

Ps 14:1   To the chief Musician, A Psalm of David.  The <u>fool</u> hath said in His heart, there is no God.  They are corrupt, they have done abominable works, there is none that doeth good.

Life outside the house of the Shepherd is a life of chaos and anxiety.  Only a <u>fool</u> would want to live apart from the house that the LORD created for mankind.  He made all things planted inside His house to flourish.  (Ps 92:12-13)  True life is found inside His House, where life outside is foolishness.  We seek to walk in His will and His wisdom.  (Eph 5:15-17)

Living inside the house and entering the kingdom is to pursue life according to the will of the Father.  Hearing and doing His Words establishes your wisdom in Him and forms your life in a house on a solid foundation. Anyone who rejects the wisdom of the LORD will be likened to a fool who built their life on the sand. (Mat 7:21-27)  His creation is His house, the "house" where we all live. We enter His house through the Door, and when we follow the "ways of His household, we find that blessing comes into our lives.  We have a choice to receive blessings or curses; life or death.  Only fools choose curses and death.....life outside.

Upon entering, learning and growing, the LORD expects us to live according to the truths that He has established for sustaining an optimum life.  It is very simple, yet profound:  To the extent we choose not to pursue His design and live outside of His house, we contribute towards the entropy of life and designate ourselves as fools.  Life in His house is doing things His way, not man's way.  He is the Way, Truth and Life  (John 14:6)

When the LORD is our shepherd, and we follow Him, He provides for us, as we walk through the valleys of life.  As we dwell in His presence, inside His house, His mercy and goodness will follow us.  Unlike the fool, we will dwell in His house forever.  (Ps 23:6)  Life outside of His house is nothing but stupidity and foolishness.

Rom 1:21-22  Because that, when they knew God, they glorified him not as God, neither were thankful; but became vain in their imaginations, and their foolish heart was darkened.  Professing themselves to be wise, they became fools,

# Free / Innocent
## Naqah

| ה | ק | נ |
|---|---|---|
| Hey | Kof | Nun |// 
| 🧍 | ⌀ | ↘ |
| Hands Up | Back of Head | Fish |
| Reveal | Follow | Life |

## Life Following The Beholding

Ps 19:12-13  Who can understand his errors? <u>cleanse</u> me from secret faults.  Keep back thy servant also from presumptuous sins; let them not have dominion over me: then shall I be upright, and I shall be <u>innocent</u> from the great transgression.

Our life of freedom and declared innocence is found when we have complete trust in His Words, for as we behold Him, He simultaneously reveals Himself to us.  During this process we grow in our liberty, realizing the reality He designed.  To live in the truth is to live in His reality, free to seek and desire His design in life, instead of man-made conclusions, that only stifle our being and freedom. Our freedom is found in trusting him with all of our heart, and not to lean on our own understanding, but to acknowledge Him in all our ways, so that He can direct our paths to follow His ways of life.  Prov 3:5-7

As we anticipate the new heavens and new earth, where His kingdom will come and His will be done in its fullest, we are declared innocent, as we behold Him and reveal Him in our lives. We live our lives according to His Word, as servants of God, not using the liberty as freedom to do what we want, but to do what He wants. This is true freedom.  (1 Peter 2:15-16) This is a life that follows and reveals true freedom in Him, because our lives are in harmony with His ways.

As we behold Him in our prayers, praise and worship, we look forward to His revelation to us, where we experience life at its fullest, forever free!  We will not misuse our freedom as a cloak of maliciousness, but as a way to serve God and our fellow man in our lives.  (1Peter 2:15-16)

The Creator and Designer of the universe gave His life for us to get our attention to the fact that His ways are the only means to freedom, liberty and innocence.  True freedom comes from beholding and revealing Him, for as we practice what He reveals to us, we will walk in the freedom He envisioned for us.  We will not recognize His instructions to us to be life restraining, but life protective and abundant.

2 Peter 3:14  Wherefore, beloved, seeing that ye look for such things, be diligent that ye may be found of Him in peace, without spot, and blameless.

# Delight
## Aneg

| ג | נ | ע |
|---|---|---|
| Gimmel | Nun | Ayin |
| ᒪ | ˋ | ⊙ |
| <u>Camel</u> | <u>Fish</u> | <u>Eye</u> |
| Lift Up | Life | See |

## See / Understand Life Lifted Up

Ps 37:4 <u>Delight</u> thyself in the LORD; and He shall give thee the desires of thine heart.

As we delight ourselves in the LORD, we understand how life is lifted up and we seek to sustain what living is all about. In doing this, the true desires of our heart will be realized and life in its fullest will be presented. Intrinsic in our heart of hearts is the desire to have the experience of life. As we present and lift up life as supreme, we find delight. The whole purpose of existence and the truth of God is to experience life and to avoid anything that diminishes life, causing chaos.

When life is pursued as a priority, everything we do will seek to bring about the original design that the LORD intended for us. His design, to lift up life, brings about peace, because it is in harmony with His will for the earth, which He created for us to enjoy forever. (Ps 37:11) Forever can only be actualized when life is pursued as a priority. Death and chaos are eliminated when life is held up as ultimate, transcending all other understanding of being.

Another picture emerges, as we delight in the LORD, and see life lifted up. His resurrection depicts the ultimate illustration of delight. In His "lifting up" we find the foundation for our delight. Without His resurrection our faith would be in vain. (1Cor 15:14-26) and there would be no hope. We understand that the purpose of His saving grace is for us to have life, and while growing in grace, grow our lives in harmony with His words, the words of life. (John 6:68) He came that we might have life and have it more abundantly. By entering into life through and with Him, we discover what life is all about and find our pasture home with Him. (John 1:9-10)

So it is, when we truly find delight, we see life lifted up and we look to do whatever we can in our lives to support the ultimate destiny of our faith; life now and life eternal. Sin destroys life, for it is not in harmony with God's will and only brings about chaos and death. When we walk in the Spirit, we live out His design for righteousness and reveal life lifted up with peace in Him, as the sons of God. (Rom 8:4-6;14)

Romans 7:22  For I delight in the law of God after the inward man.

# Hear / Obey / Harken
# Shama

| ע | מ | שׁ |
|---|---|---|
| Ayin | Mem | Shin |

| 👁 | 〰 | ⊔⊔ |
|---|---|---|
| Eye | Water | Teeth |
| Understand | Chaos | Destroy |

## Destruction of Chaos Understood

Deut 6:4-6 Hear, O Israel: The LORD our God is one LORD. And thou shalt love the LORD thy God with all thine heart, and with all thy soul, and with all thy might. And these words, which I command thee this day, shall be in thine heart.

One of the greatest monumental events in history, revisited for the people of God to uphold, commenced with the directive to hear what was said. Yahshua (Jesus) also referenced this quote from Deuteronomy, as admonition to obey the greatest commandment given by God. Hearing God's Words are followed by doing.

Hearing and doing what is instructed is implied, especially when it is God's Word "speaking" to us. When we pray, we ask the LORD to hear our prayers. Inferred in our requests to the LORD is that the LORD take action; not only to hear our prayers, but to do something.

The LORD told us that His Words are Spirit and life. As we read His Word and our heart hears the Words of life, we are moved to keep His ways. He puts His Words and Spirit within us, by writing them on our hearts in the renewed covenant promise. (John 6:63; Ez 36:27; Jer 31:31-33) Listening, hearing, doing are all interrelated, for if one chooses not to do, he/she has not heard the Words of the LORD, and/or is choosing to be rebellious. (Ez 31:12)

The fruit of hearing His Words is living in the Spirit. By living according to His Words, we will produce the fruit of the Spirit in our daily walk. Heaven mingles with earth when the Spirit flows into our lives through hearing and harkening to His voice. (Gal 5:22-25)

The greatest commandment for living begins with hearing, followed by our doing. The fruit of our lives is revealed in what we think, say and do. We see throughout scripture that blessing comes with doing what is said, and not by only hearing. Thus, we need to put the Words of our faith into action to complete the blessing.

The destruction of the chaos around us can only be eliminated by first hearing the Words of the LORD and then applying the Words to our lives.

James 1:22 But be ye doers of the word, and not hearers only, deceiving your own selves.

# Spirit / Breath / Wind
# Ruwach

| ח | ו | ר |
|---|---|---|
| Chet | Vav | Resh |
| 🧱 | Y | 𐤓 |
| <u>Wall</u> | <u>Nail</u> | <u>Head</u> |
| Protection | Connect | Thoughts |

## Head's Connection to Protection

Psalm 51:10-11   Create in me a clean heart, O God; and renew a right <u>spirit</u> within me.  Cast me not away from thy presence; and take not thy holy <u>spirit</u> from me.

An awesome picture is given to us about one of the most vital activities we can practice when living in the Spirit.  Keeping the thoughts in our heads connected to His protection is both an essential and beautiful picture of our walk with The LORD.  We need to stay connected!!!

As we contemplate His Word in our moment by moment decisions, we remain connected to the protection He provides through His Spirit.  A very key aspect of a successful walk in the Spirit is to stay connected to activate love, joy, peace, longsuffering, gentleness, goodness, faith, meekness, and temperance.  (Gal 5:22-23)

As the seed of the Holy Word takes root in our hearts, the fruit we produce will be characterized and identified as being the fruit of the Holy Spirit. The Word of God produces the fruit of the Spirit, as we consciously live out the Words of life. It is through a deliberate awareness and application of the seeds of God's Word that produces fruit in our walk with the Spirit. (Gal 5:16, 25)

Vital to our physical life is each breath we take. Essential to our spiritual being is the Spirit of the LORD, living in our hearts, protecting us and giving us the breath of life. Our lives cannot continue without breathing the air our physical bodies need to exist. Air is critical to our existence. The LORD's design is that air be moved through our lungs and absorbed, so our flesh can be sustained. Likewise, the Spirit is critical for our spiritual beings to survive.

Only by connecting with Him do we find protection, for in His Words we find life. His Words provide us with guidance on how to live our lives; "living in the Spirit". The whole principle of living in the Spirit is found in the very word itself: Spirit. While we apply His Words and principles during our daily moment by moment walk, we truly keep the thoughts in our heads connected to the protection that He provides for us.

John 6:63 It is the spirit that quickeneth; the flesh profiteth nothing: the words that I speak unto you, they are spirit, and they are life.

# Mind / Imagination / Mold
## Yetser / Yatsar

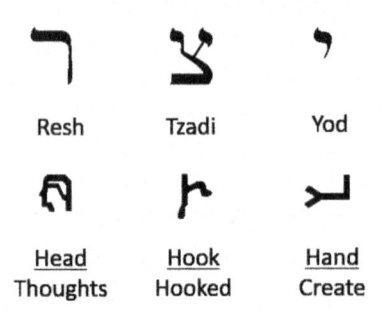

| ר | צ | י |
|---|---|---|
| Resh | Tzadi | Yod |
| ᕽ | ᖌ | ᒧ |
| <u>Head</u> | <u>Hook</u> | <u>Hand</u> |
| Thoughts | Hooked | Create |

## Hand Hooked to your Thoughts

Isaiah 26:3  Thou wilt keep him in perfect peace, whose <u>mind</u> is stayed on thee: because he trusteth in thee.

Peace comes to our being when we focus our thoughts on the "right" things. By having our minds stayed on the "things of the LORD", we eliminate the concepts and behaviors connected to chaos we create in our lives.

There is a natural progression from thought, to word, unto action. This sequence is highly influenced by what we look at, listen to, talk about, and do. All that we do is based on what goes on in our heads. Thus our hands (what we do) originates from the thoughts in our heads. Everything we think/do either enhances or impairs life. Thus, our hands are hooked to our heads. What are our heads hooked to?

Our head needs to remain connected to the Holy Spirit for our protection. It is in the Spirit where we find the words and concepts forming the activities of life. It is very interesting to note that the Hebrew word "Potter" is the same as the word imagination. The "Potter" forms the clay from the imagination within his mind and heart. We also form the activities in our lives with our hands joined to the imagination of our minds. He is the Potter and we are the clay. (Isa 64:8) As we live our lives, we pray that the words we speak and the meditation of our hearts are acceptable to Him. (Ps 19:14) We do not want to be hard clay, but soft and pliable in His hands, for then He can mold our hearts and minds and be the Shepherd of the house where we live.

Being the Shepherd of our house, we give Him authority over our hearts. As our hearts are molded, we do what is in harmony with His will. Everything we think, say and do, will be in harmony with His Spirit and will bear fruit for the kingdom. Kingdom living is keeping our beliefs and subsequent actions in sync with Him.

Living in the Spirit is when our thoughts and meditation on the Word develop into blessed imagination and action. The more our minds are stayed on His Words, we become clay in His hands and we form the "mind of Messiah". (John 6:63; 1 Cor 2:12-16)

Phil 2:5 Let this mind be in you, which was also in Christ Jesus. ((Yahshua Ha'Mashiach))

# Comfort
## Nacham

| מ | ח | נ |
|---|---|---|
| Mem | Chet | Nun |
| 〰 | ⬛ | ⵏ |
| Water | Wall | Fish |
| Chaos | Protect | Life |

## Life Protected from Chaos

Isaiah 51:3   For the LORD shall comfort Zion: he will comfort all her waste places; and he will make her wilderness like Eden, and her desert like the garden of the LORD; joy and gladness shall be found therein, thanksgiving, and the voice of melody.

Yes, when that day of comfort comes, mankind will experience what life is like without chaos in the world. The LORD describes comfort as "life protected from chaos". We can see glimpses of this reality today when we are somewhat insulated from situations going on in the world.

Our comfort is most readily experienced when we follow His Words of life. His Words of life are opposed to the chaos around us. He gives us guidance and instruction as to how we should live….. what we should do within His design.

We are comforted as we walk in this life through all of the turmoil, realizing that He is with us and His rod and staff comfort us, even in the valleys and shadows in this world system. (Ps 23:4) Being His sheep, we follow His voice, as he prods us, so that we stay on the path of life. Following Him keeps us as safe as possible, and as comfortable as possible, given the circumstances that surround us.

Only the LORD can provide us with comfort in our lives now and ultimate comfort when He returns. We should not look to mankind for our crucial safety and security, but to the LORD only, for He is our maker and shepherd. We need to see His hand and fear Him alone. (Isa 51:12-13) Providing us with the comfort and assurance of a mother (a beautiful picture), He has promised to comfort us. (Isa 66:13-14)

The more we follow His words of truth, life on earth can temporarily be a beautiful place of comfort in Him. With Him abiding in us, we are protected from chaos, while we wait for the blessed hope of His return. (Titus 2:11-15) True comfort comes by the Holy Spirit living in us.

John 14:16-18  And I will pray the Father, and he shall give you another Comforter, that he may abide with you for ever; even the Spirit of truth; whom the world cannot receive, because it sees him not, neither knoweth him: but ye know him; for he dwelleth with you, and shall be in you. I will not leave you comfortless: I will come to you.

# Assembly / Congregation
## Kahal

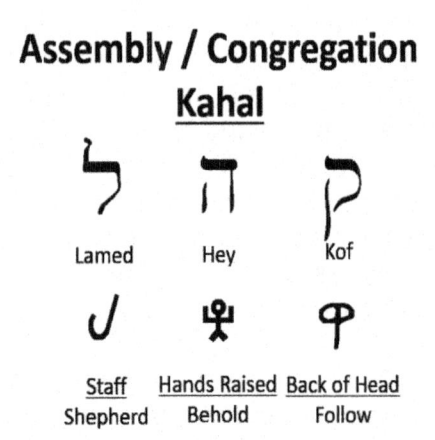

ל　ה　ק
Lamed　Hey　Kof

Staff　Hands Raised　Back of Head
Shepherd　Behold　Follow

## Following, Beholding The Shepherd

Psalms 40:10  I have not hid thy righteousness within my heart; I have declared thy faithfulness and thy salvation: I have not concealed thy lovingkindness and thy truth from the great congregation.

People come together upon hearing the voice of the Good shepherd. When hearing and beholding Him, we assemble together in fellowship and praise to His honor and glory. This "place" is an experience and is not referring to a building, but to a relationship with Him and with those who follow Him. This original concept of assembly can be seen in the modern phrase, "birds of a feather, flock together". Yes, we come together, seeking and praising Him, as we behold the wonders of His creation. (Ps 89:5)

As we study His word and behold His voice,

we can identify with the spiritual truth that we are His sheep and we follow Him, because we recognize His voice from the scriptures. He is the Good Shepherd and the door to the sheepfold. Inside the door to the sheepfold we find our brothers and sisters, who are also seeking a relationship with the Shepherd of life's beautiful pasture. (John 10:1-18) He has told us that He is the way, the truth and the life. (John 14:6) Our life will be blessed, when we follow His design, as we reveal His truth in our lives.

As we follow and behold the Shepherd, we are changed. Beholding Him in fellowship, with our brothers and sisters in the LORD, provides us with a community of faith that will strengthen and preserve us, as we walk in the Spirit of liberty in Him. (2 Cor 3:17-18) We are transformed by following His voice, renewing our minds, and leaving the ways of the world, while learning the will of God in communion with Him. (Rom 12:2) By beholding we experience the kingdom.

We of like mind assemble together when beholding the Shepherd. What follows is the result of Him revealing and us following the Truth of His Word .....His following.....His assembly! As true followers, we are not hearers only, but doers of the Word. (James 1:21-25)

1 Tim 3:15 But if I tarry long, that thou mayest know how thou oughtest to behave thyself in the house of God, which is the church of the living God, the pillar and ground of the truth.

# Laudation / Praise / Hymn
## Tahillah

| ה | ל | ה | ת |
|---|---|---|---|
| Hey | Lamed | Hey | Tav |
| 🧍 | ✔ | 🧍 | † |
| Hands Raised | Staff | Hands Raised | Cross |
| Reveal | Shepherd | Reveal | Covenant |

## Covenant Revealed Shepherd Revealed

Psalm 79:13   So we thy people and sheep of thy pasture will give thee thanks for ever; we will shew forth thy praise to all generations.

Upon hearing His voice we follow Him and realize the blessings that are found in His pasture.  The covenant and Shepherd of the covenant are revealed to us, whereby we give thanks and praise to His name.  In His pasture we discover the depth, richness and beauty of His creation and His role in the plan of salvation.

As we feed upon the spiritual food He provides, we begin to understand His grace toward us and our need to follow His words of life.  When we comprehend the awesome impact to our lives and the eternal destiny that is given to us, we sing, we praise, and express our joy in song, because we receive a glimpse of His plan and breathtaking glory.

As the whole eternal meaning of the covenant is unfolded to us, we can't help but express our joy in songs of praise. We begin to understand what the sign of the covenant means to our future. In connecting our thoughts to the sScriptures and studying His ways, we build our beliefs on His Word. Our beliefs develop into a trust and form a set apart attitude toward life, as we abide in Him. Our attitude then directs our actions, when repeated over time, becomes the habits we cultivate. All of the above combined, forms our character and reveals our destiny. All of this is expressed in our praise and manifestation of our lives in covenant with the LORD. (Ps 40:3)

To know that our destiny is with the Shepherd, because we have faith in the Covenant, is a beautiful experience to take with us each moment of the day, while growing in the awareness and design of His kingdom. (Deut 26:18-19)

We show forth His praise and bring honor to Him every time we reveal the covenant and demonstrate how the Shepherd works in our lives. Earth's garden will spring forth, as we grow in His righteousness and give Him praise, as a witness to all nations. (Isa 61:10-11)

Hebrews 2:12 Saying, I will declare thy name unto my brethren, in the midst of the church will I sing praise unto thee.

# Bride
## Kallah

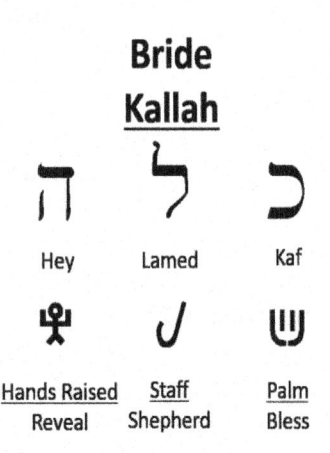

ה ל כ

Hey     Lamed     Kaf

Hands Raised     Staff     Palm
Reveal     Shepherd     Bless

## Blessings of The Shepherd Revealed

Isaiah 61:10   I will greatly rejoice in the LORD, my soul shall be joyful in my God; for he hath clothed me with the garments of salvation, he hath covered me with the robe of righteousness, as a bridegroom decketh himself with ornaments, and as a bride adorneth herself with her jewels.

Blessings by the shepherd are revealed when we are in relationship with Him.  Rejoicing in the LORD and finding joy in God are an outward sign of our bond with Him.  The bride is presented as being clothed with the garments of salvation and being covered with the robe of righteousness.  Life as a bride illustrates the most beautiful relationship one can experience.  A bride is analogous to the plan of redemption, when the text references salvation and righteousness.  Living in grace and following

His ways reveal our relationship to Him, as an illustration of the love commitment between the bride and husband. In our current bride and bridegroom relationships, we can experience a glimpse of this oneness with our God when we are "one flesh" together.

All through the history of mankind, the scriptures illustrate the relationship between the LORD and His assembly (church) of believers. He has picked the bride and bridegroom as the way to demonstrate our love for Him and our love for each other. Within the structure of a husband and wife, He has given us the opportunity to grow and learn what love means as the members of His body of believers. (Eph 5:30-33) The blessings of the Shepherd are revealed as jewels and ornaments, when we live out a true love relationship with our spouse.

The ultimate and final fulfillment regarding the plan of salvation, for those married to the "Lamb of God", will be to experience the eternal destiny of a beautiful life of peace, joy, and happiness, without any chaos, pain or death. The new heavens and new earth are illustrated for us in the context of a bride, living in oneness with her husband. It is a beautiful picture the LORD has created to exemplify the essence of a bride, when He shows us that the blessings of the Shepherd are revealed through her.

Rev 21:9b "Come hither, I will shew thee the bride, the Lamb's wife."

# Oil / Shine
## Shemen

| נ | מ | שׁ |
|---|---|---|
| Nun | Mem | Shin |// (Fish/Life) (Water/Chaos) (Teeth/Destroy)

Nun — Fish / Life
Mem — Water / Chaos
Shin — Teeth / Destroy

## Destroy the Chaos in Life

Ps 23:5b-6 …thou anointest my head with oil; my cup runneth over. Surely goodness and mercy shall follow me all the days of my life: and I will dwell in the house of the LORD for ever.

We are set apart through the anointing oil and are uniquely prepared to bring goodness and mercy to those with whom we engage in life's journey. As we dwell in the House of the LORD, our mission is to destroy the chaos in life by the sweet fragrance we emit to others.

We find Oil in the Scriptures revealed in many ways. Oil, with its many applications, smooths, heals, shines, scents, anoints and provides fuel for light. Its purpose is to destroy the chaos in life, when used as designed.

Many events in life require oil. When we need to

take the "rough edges" out of a situation or when there is conflict and strife, oil can be used to sooth a struggle.  When applying oil to our lives, we can smooth the roughness and allow the oil to remove the friction.  We are the vessels that hold the oil and should be ready to apply it at any given moment.

As was the practice in the temple, so are we to keep oil in our lamps day and night.  (Ex 27:20) As the temple of the Holy Spirit, we must be equipped at all times to live and give light. (1 Cor 3:16)  When we have enough oil, we can keep our lamps lit, live in the light, see the chaos of life around us, and avoid the darkness. When one is experiencing discouragement, this form of darkness is depressing.  Living in the light diminishes the chaos that surround us, as darkness cannot coexist with light.

Wisdom in life is understood and experienced in the light.  When we live in the light, we come to be a reflection of that light, being filled with oil, becoming a light to the world.  (Mat 5:14)  Oil provides the fuel to keep our candles emitting light, thus destroying the chaos around us.

Mat 25:1-4  Then shall the kingdom of heaven be likened unto ten virgins, which took their lamps, and went forth to meet the bridegroom. And five of them were wise, and five were foolish.  They that were foolish took their lamps, and took no oil with them:  But the wise took oil in their vessels with their lamps.

## Light
## 'Owr

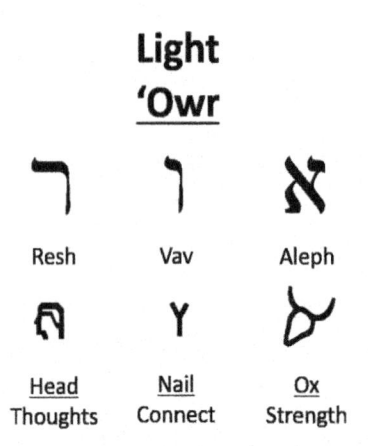

| ר | ו | א |
|---|---|---|
| Resh | Vav | Aleph |
| ᚱ | Y | ᛒ |
| Head | Nail | Ox |
| Thoughts | Connect | Strength |

## Strength Connected to the Head

Ps 119:105   NUN. Thy word is a lamp unto my feet, and a light unto my path.

Our thoughts are strengthened and power is realized in our being via the brain inside of our heads. The brain is where our mind resides. In order to see and understand reality, our "mind's eye" located in our head, requires light to function effectively and accurately.

The ability to see the creation through the perspective of God's Word provides us light. This light is the power needed to see reality. Reality is truth. (John 17:17) Light is needed to see in the physical realm and to understand what we see spiritually. The Word of God is the source of light and reflects in our understanding of life and behavior toward others. (John 8:12) In His light we shall see light, as He is the fountain of life. (Ps 36:9) The ultimate strength of a person is to live in the light and to be a light to the world. The Lord told us that we also are a light of the world and we are to let our lights shine, as we follow Him. (Mat 5:14-16)

The key question in life is, do we see what we understand or do we understand what we see? Understanding what we see can only be found in the light of His Word, for only there can we find the strength and insight that is connected to our being. (Ps 119:130) Can you imagine yourself living in complete darkness? Without the light of His Word, one lives in the dark and cannot see what is really happening in the world. The light of His Word guides us through life and provides us with the insight to truly see the path we are following.

Light and understanding goes beyond seeing the past and present circumstances of life. The light of His Word also provides us with insight into future developments coming on the world stage, while the "grand finale" is accomplished. Light will provide us with the understanding we need. By reflecting the Light of His Word, we can connect to the powerful light provided for our thoughts, our minds and our being.

2 Peter 1:19  We have also a more sure word of prophecy; whereunto ye do well that ye take heed, as unto a light that shineth in a dark place, until the day dawn, and the day star arise in your hearts:

# Shadow
## Tsel

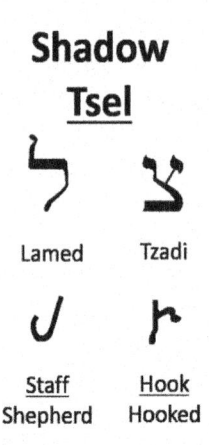

לצ

Lamed    Tzadi

Staff    Hook
Shepherd    Hooked

## Hooked to The Shepherd

Ps 36:7 How excellent is thy lovingkindness, O God! therefore the children of men put their trust under the <u>shadow</u> of thy wings.

In His shadow means that we are living close to Him. Alive under the shadow of His wings is a direct picture of our being when we live mindful of the LORD, "hooked" to Him, emulating everything He does. Being so close, living in His shadow, illustrates our desire and passion for Him, because we watch His every move in order to remain in His presence; in His shadow.

Many places in scripture identify His presence and living in His shadow as being under His wings. (Ps 17:8; 63:7) When the light of His Word shines and we abide with Him by following His Word, we live in the secret place of the Most High.

Living close to Him in this His shadow provides us with a refuge and fortress. (Ps 91:1-4) The secret place of the Most High means that we dwell in Him with complete trust in His ability to deliver us when in His presence.

There are many examples in reality that we see every day demonstrating what a shadow does. Simply spoken, a shadow takes on the direct form of the object it represents. In addition to the main object casting the shadow, a shadow needs light in order to be created.

The Lamb of God is a major theme of the scriptures. "Behold the Lamb of God who takes away the sin of the world." (John 1:29) What does a lamb have to do with anything? Only by understanding the shape and presentation of the Lamb's shadow in the Old Testament, can accurately identify the fulfilment and meaning presented in the New Testament. The Lamb has a significant role and place in our faith and is only understood and identified by the Passover Lamb and sacrifices in the scriptures.

When reading the Old Testament we see many shadows providing a portrayal of the LORD with events to come. Identify and understand His shadow pictures, as created by the light of His Word, and know you are "hooked" to the Good Shepherd. Live a blessed life in His shadow.

Col 2:17 Which are a shadow of things to come; but the body is of Christ.

# See / Behold
## Ra'ah

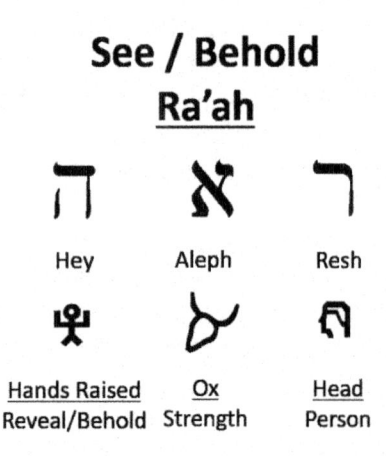

| הֵ | א | ר |
|---|---|---|
| Hey | Aleph | Resh |
| Hands Raised<br>Reveal/Behold | Ox<br>Strength | Head<br>Person |

## Head's Strength Revealed

Isa 41:20   That they may see, and know, and consider, and understand together, that the hand of the LORD hath done this, and the Holy One of Israel hath created it.

The strength of a person's sight is revealed when understanding and knowledge is examined in the context of the creator. The absolute power of our sense of sight is found when we see everything through His revelation. It is a blessing to see the creation around you. The mind, when connected to the light of the Word, can go beyond seeing only, but to understanding what one sees. Those not following and rebelling against the Word of God have eyes to see, but see not. (Eze 12:2)

After coming to the LORD, we need to keep our eyes open, staying aware of what is going on around us. We received our "wake up" call and it is time to walk circumspectly, not as fools, but as wise, because he woke us up from the dead. We can truly see, for now we are alert with our eyes open, walking in His light. (Eph 5:13-15)

Even when reading the happenings in the current news, we perceive the signs of the times that were written in the Scriptures for us to discover. We see the fig tree and know that summer is near, even at the doors. (Mat 24:32-33) Also, we recognize that we are living in the last days, as we can see the events developing all around us. We are able to observe these things, because we live in the light of His Word with the darkness removed.

The strength of our head is revealed with our eyes, having the ability to see beyond the physical world. In order to fully develop our eyesight, we need to be born again of the Spirit. By seeing His kingdom, we can understand life and identify our purpose. Only by dying and being born again of the Spirit can we see and discern spiritual things. Having insight into His kingdom, through the light of His Word, provides us with the vision of His realm. (Mat 13:16)

Seeing in the natural is a blessing in itself, but to also see spiritually is truly revealing the strength and power of our heads, as He intended.

John 3:3b ... I say unto thee, Except a man be born again, he cannot see the kingdom of God.

# Good / Goodness
# Towb

| ב | ו | ט |
|---|---|---|
| Bet | Vav | Tet |
| ⌐┘ | Y | ⊗ |
| House<br>Inside | Nail<br>Attach | Basket<br>Surround |

## Surrounded, Attached to The House

Ps 23:6  Surely goodness and mercy shall follow me all the days of my life: and I will dwell in the house of the LORD for ever.

Being surrounded and connected to the house of the LORD is a blessing. When living inside His house we experience life as He created it. We realize that His ways are His design for life. Living in His house means that we honor "House Rules". Not killing, not stealing and the other life instructions He gave us are for our own good.

His will be done on earth, as it is in heaven, is our desire when seeking His kingdom and goodness in life. (Mat 6:10) Biblical principles govern our behavior, as the way, the truth, and the life in His kingdom. (Jn 14:6) Following His design, the way to live, the way He created it, is to live in His house, where goodness is found.

He created goodness to be the kingdom's framework.  Living in His house transforms us out of the world, moving us to do what He has established, as His good and perfect will.  (Rom 12:2)  By choosing to enter into His domain, we are renewed and find the blessings that He intended for us to be realized in life.  We find the true beauty He intended for us to experience, when we dwell in His house and are surrounded by our conscious awareness of Him.   (Ps 27:4)

The only entrance to the Father's house is through the door.  (Jn 10:7-11)  Entering through the door of the Good Shepherd, we find abundant life.  Dwelling in His house we find true understanding, knowing that His house was created to produce and sustain life.

When we live in His house we honor His ways and trust in Him.  He invites us to live in His presence and to enjoy the blessing of creation as He designed.  (Ps 34:8)  Living in the Spirit is to live in His house by walking in the Spirit, producing the fruit of the Spirit and knowing that we are dwelling inside of the House He created.  We experience the ultimate blessings that life has to offer when we are surrounded, connected to His House and we are aware of our surroundings moment by moment.

Gal 5:22-23   But the fruit of the Spirit is love, joy, peace, longsuffering, gentleness, goodness, faith, Meekness, temperance: against such there is no law.

# Meditate / Imagine
# Hagah

הּ　　גּ　　הּ

Hey　　Gimmel　　Hey

☥　　L　　☥

Hands Raised　Camel　Hands Raised
Revealing　　Lift Up　　Beholding

## Behold, Lift Up and Reveal

Ps 143:5-6  I remember the days of old; I meditate on all thy works; I muse on the work of thy hands.  I stretch forth my hands unto thee: my soul thirsteth after thee, as a thirsty land. Selah.

Meditation is a beautiful state of mind to pursue. The principal inspiration behind the word Hagah can be found in the Paleo letters that form the word.  To behold, lift up and reveal, outlines the complete process intended by this reflection.

True meditation is initiated by beholding the LORD's Word, presenting yourself to Him, and completing the process by revealing Him to others through your example of what you say and do in life.  By beholding we become changed, is a Biblical principle that shines forth from this word, Hagah.  As it says in 2 Cor 3:18, by beholding the glory of the LORD, we are changed. As we meditate on His word and lift up our thoughts to Him, we reveal Him when we allow His Spirit to direct our lives. He told us that His words are Spirit and they are life. When we produce the fruit of the Spirit, we express our awareness of Him in what we say and do, while thinking on these things. (Phil 4:8-9)

We are admonished to be doers of the Word and not hearers only. (Jam 1:23-25) There is liberty in life when we come to the realization that His words of instruction produce blessing. The blessings of His word in our lives are realized by us, and also, by those around us. We reveal Him, not only by what we say, but primarily by what we do with the Spirit living in us.

Meditation, in its truest sense, is a moment by moment experience. As we are aware, and consciously live in His presence, our state of mind is connected to Him, beholding Him in our imaginations. As we present ourselves to Him, we connect to His Spirit, revealing him in our behavior, which is the whole purpose and design of meditation. Reflective mindfulness of the Scriptures is the foundation for meditation.

1 Tim 4:15-16 Meditate upon these things; give thyself wholly to them; that thy profiting may appear to all. Take heed unto thyself, and unto the doctrine; continue in them: for in doing this thou shalt both save thyself, and them that hear thee.

# Wait / Patience / Expectation
## Qavah

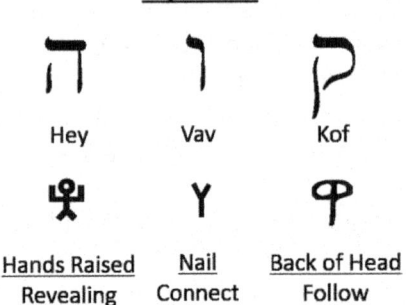

| ה | ו | ק |
|---|---|---|
| Hey | Vav | Kof |
| Hands Raised | Nail | Back of Head |
| Revealing | Connect | Follow |

## What Follows Connecting, Beholding

Isaiah 25:9   And it shall be said in that day, Lo, this is our God; we have waited for him, and he will save us: this is the LORD; we have waited for him, we will be glad and rejoice in his salvation.

As we behold Him and reveal Him in our lives, we complete the idea presented in the word picture, QAVAH.  Following His ways, through connecting to Him, we establish Him in our daily walk.  This expectation develops and nurtures the blessed hope that we have in our salvation.

As can be perceived in many examples found in the scriptures, His timing is not always ours.  We are admonished to "wait upon the LORD" and put our trust in Him.  As we study His word and develop an understanding of His truth, we come to realize that He is in control and it is all about

His timing. Our patience is developed and strengthened as we study His word. (Ps 135:5) So, in the context of this word, QAVAH, what follows is connecting and beholding Him in our lives, revealing His influence on our behavior.

We renew our strength each day in this life by following, connecting and beholding the LORD. (Isa 40:31) He is our refuge and strength in all circumstances. (Ps 46:1) In times of plenty and trouble we find our salvation in Him, as we seek His truth and are taught His ways, while waiting for His complete revelation. (Ps 25:5)

The scriptures were written for our learning, so that we may have hope in this life, in expectation for the life to come. (Rom 15:4) During this time we are comforted by the scriptures, experiencing patience through the fruit of the Spirit. We grow and reveal Him, as we behold and connect with His will, wisdom and understanding. (Col 1:9-13)

We wait on the LORD in earnest expectation as we follow, connect, and behold Him. When we read His word and contemplate His ways, we trust in Him for what we do not see. We wait for the completed manifestation of His word to be revealed in our lives with hope and patience.

Rom 8:24-25  For we are saved by hope: but hope that is seen is not hope: for what a man seeth, why doth he yet hope for? But if we hope for that we see not, then do we with patience wait for it.

# Remember / Mindful
## Zachar

ר     כ     ז

Resh     Kaf     Zayin

| Head | Palm | Tool |
|---|---|---|
| Thoughts | Give | Cut |

## Etch What's Given Into Thoughts

Ps 25:6-7 Remember, O LORD, thy tender mercies and thy lovingkindnesses; for they have been ever of old. Remember not the sins of my youth, nor my transgressions: according to thy mercy remember thou me for thy goodness' sake, O LORD.

The fruit of what one does and says is a result of connecting with one's memory. When the LORD said He would not remember our sins and iniquities no more (Heb 8:12), He was advising us that He was not going to take action with respect to that knowledge, even though, as God, He would still be aware of the fact of our sin.

To remember is to take action with regard to that knowledge. Zachar means that the thought is firmly planted into our being, such that we respond according to our heart's understanding.

The LORD desires us to etch His words into our thoughts in such a way that we, not only recall what he has said, but we also act in harmony with that recall and knowledge. Being mindful of something is a conscious awareness of a concept that is put into action when needed.

Somewhere, at some time, we have been given a thought, planted it and now choose to act on it, or not. Zachar, the action of being mindful or to recall something, becomes remembering, when we respond with intent to fulfil the recollection. It is very important that we fill our heads with His words, so we can remember His ways, meaning that we put His words into action. (Ps 77:11-12)

Being conscious of the LORD's presence is a form of being attentive of Him. When we can keep Him in our thoughts and act in unity with His word, we enter into an awareness of His kingdom. In our everyday lives we put our trust in His name and call out to Him, because we remember Him. (Ps 20:6-9) His name is etched into our thoughts and we are mindful of Him.

As we remember and grow in His forgiveness, we think of His covenant. We will desire His ways and His laws will be written in our hearts.

Heb 10:16-17 This is the covenant that I will make with them after those days, saith the Lord, I will put my laws into their hearts, and in their minds will I write them; And their sins and iniquities will I remember no more.

# Hope / Trust / Wait
## Yachal

| ל | ח | י |
|---|---|---|
| Lamed | Chet | Yod |
| Staff | Wall | Hand |
| Shepherd | Protect | Do |

## The Hand of Protection with The Shepherd

Ps 42:5  Why art thou cast down, O my soul? And why art thou disquieted in me?  hope thou in God:  for I shall yet praise him for the help of his countenance.

When we are with the Shepherd we can have hope and trust in His protection.  Being aware of His presence provides us with the spiritual help we need, as we wait on Him.  Trusting Him is an essential practice for living our lives with Him.  He directs us to be of good courage when facing the challenges of life.  He will strengthen our hearts, as we hope in Him.  (Ps 31:24)

Beholding the hand of the LORD and fearing Him gives us hope, knowing that He sees us and will have mercy on us.  The "hand that we see" should be His hand in all things, as He is in ultimate control, and will be our help and our shield, as we wait on Him.  (Ps 33:18-20)

Being protected by the Shepherd means that we have a wall of protection. We stand fortified in Him, as we depend on Him as our fortress. He is our strength and we trust in Him. He is our Rock. (Ps 18:2)

Like Abraham, we all need to wait obediently to receive the promises of God. We anticipate the blessed hope and the glorious appearing of our Savior. (Titus 2:13) In that expectation we wait patiently for the inheritance that is promised to us. (Heb 6:11-15) In the mean time we will find peace for our souls by resting in His words and through staying attached to the vine. He is the vine and we are the branches. (Jn 15:1-8) By holding on to the vine, we get our nourishment and strength to trust, as we walk through the valleys and navigate the mountains of this world.

We live our days clasping His hand, and by holding on to Him, we choose to live under His protection. Only He can provide us with the ultimate expectation of a magnificent future, as assured in His word, while we walk with Him.

Yachal; hoping, trusting, and waiting under His shelter is a comforting feeling. Believing, we put our confidence in His ways, and trust through the power of the Holy Spirit. In the hope, only He can provide, do we find peace and joy.

Rom 15:13 Now the God of hope fill you with all joy and peace in believing, that ye may abound in hope, through the power of the Holy Ghost.

# Rock / Fortress
## Cela

| ע | ל | ס |
|---|---|---|
| Ayin | Lamed | Samech |

| 👁 | 𐤋 | ₹ |
|---|---|---|
| <u>Eye</u> | <u>Staff</u> | <u>Prop</u> |
| Understand | Shepherd | Support |

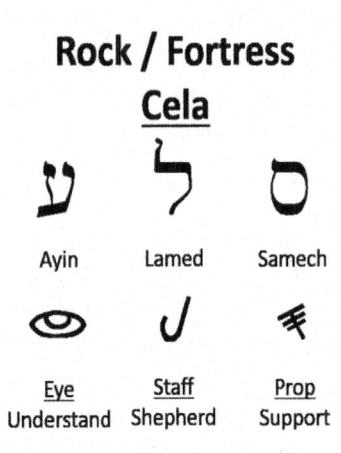

## Supported by The Shepherd's Understanding

Ps 31:3   For thou art my <u>rock</u> and my fortress; therefore for thy name's sake lead me, and guide me.

We stand firmly upon the Rock when we depend on and are supported by what The Shepherd sees and understands.  The words of The Shepherd give us the ability to comprehend reality, by providing us with a firm foundation to stand upon.  He will lead and guide us, as we lean on Him………. our fortress.

Throughout the Scriptures the LORD has admonished us to hear and to do the Words He has spoken.  It is in the hearing of His Word, with doing, that we stand on the rock He has provided for us.  If we lean not on our own understanding, but acknowledge Him, the LORD will be able to direct our paths.  (Prov 3:5-6)

The present-day culture we live in today has perverted many of the basic fundamentals of truth. While what we choose to do, may not be popular in the culture, we can have the assurance, that He is our habitation and our fortress. (Ps 71:3) We can stand on His principles for our life's journey and look to Him in whom we trust. We choose to live in His kingdom, for eventually His will, will be done on earth, as it is in heaven. His reality is the foundation Rock of life, as His design is the basis of all existence.

The scriptures demonstrate that the foundational principle of our beliefs is founded in the Messiah, the Rock of our faith. Both in the Hebrew Scriptures and in the New Testament Scriptures we find our knowledge and understanding by standing on the Rock. (1 Cor 10:4; Mat 16:18)

In doing life His way, we discover The Way, The Truth and The Life. We truly are supported by His understanding, when we depend on The Shepherd's wisdom in all things. You have probably heard it sung......"On the solid Rock we stand, all other ground is sinking sand."

Mat 7:24,26   Therefore whosoever heareth these sayings of mine, and doeth them, I will liken him unto a wise man, which built his house upon a rock: And every one that heareth these sayings of mine, and doeth them not, shall be likened unto a foolish man, which built his house upon the sand:

# Faithful / Believe
## Aman

| Nun | Mem | Aleph |
|---|---|---|
| Fish | Water | Ox |
| Life | Chaos | First |

Em / Mother

## Mother of Life / Give Birth to Life

Ps 31:23   O love the LORD, all ye his saints: for the LORD preserveth the faithful, and plentifully rewardeth the proud doer.

We are rewarded and preserved by being faithful. What gives birth to life is a mother. Life from "first water". What can be a more perfect example of being faithful, than that of a mother? What nurtures life is belief and true faithfulness.

A mother is revealed in her motherhood. Faith is borne out by what we are faithful to and by what we believe to be reality or truth. When we decide to believe in the LORD, we follow His ways and look to do anything that supports and sustains life. Upholding life is what it is all about. A mother does everything to safeguard and protect the life of her child in every situation and circumstance she experiences in life.

Faith is action and good works; believing is not only head knowledge. We have faith in the Word and believe in the LORD for His salvation, by being faithful to His Words. Faith without works is dead. (Jam 2:18, 20) We express our works and choose to do His commandments, not to be saved, for we cannot be justified by our works, for we are saved by grace through faith. Because of grace, being saved, we choose to live according to His Words, unto good works, and walk according to what He has ordained to be the way to live, nurturing life. (Eph 2:8-10)

The scriptures show us that faith comes by hearing and hearing by the word of God. (Rom 10:17) We find substance and meaning in God's word, giving us solid counsel on how to manifest life. Being a believer is not only having an intellectual understanding about the Bible, but it is demonstrated by nurturing, walking and living out what one believes and recognizes to be true.

The evidence of our faith is established and nurtured in life on earth, by experiencing our faithfulness. We overcome the world through His Word living in our lives, being believers and victorious doers of our faith. Now, being born again by His Word, the normal thing for us to do is to nurture the life He has given us, as a mother nurtures her baby.

1 Jn 5:4  For whatsoever is born of God overcometh the world: and this is the victory that overcometh the world, even our faith.

# Righteousness / Righteous
## Tsedeq

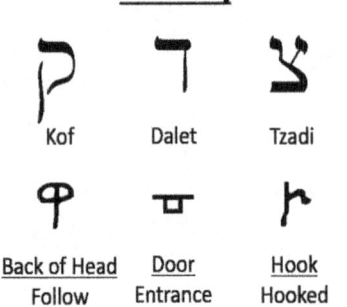

| ק | ד | צ |
|---|---|---|
| Kof | Dalet | Tzadi |

| Back of Head | Door | Hook |
|---|---|---|
| Follow | Entrance | Hooked |

## Hooked to The Door and Following

Ps 23:3   He restoreth my soul: he leadeth me in the paths of righteousness for his name's sake.

We are hooked to the door as we follow Him and we are led in the path of righteousness.  When being hooked to Him, following His ways, we represent Him, and do what we can do to bring honor and glory to Him for His name's sake.

Due to His death and resurrection on our behalf, we now, through faith in what He did, choose to live according to His ways.  We don't make void the law through our faith, we establish the law, (Rom 3:31) not to be saved, but because we are saved, we choose to live in harmony with Him.

The justification that comes by faith cannot be earned by living a righteous life.  Living righteously is a result of our realization of the grace bestowed upon us. We grow in grace through sanctification, being justified by faith in Him. Having a passion for Him, we follow His ways, as revealed in His word. (1 Pet 1:2)

We, through the Spirit, wait for the hope of righteousness by faith. (Gal 5:5) We now live hooked to Him, The door, growing in the faith Messiah has given us through the power of His resurrection. It is not through the works of the law that saves us, but through our faith we are justified before God. (Gal 2:16) With the new covenant written on our hearts, we choose to live agreeing to His law, because we know that His Word is truth and we want to live in harmony with Him. (Jer 3:31) By faith, which gives birth to life, we understand that the Creator knows what is best for us. His Words are Spirit and His Words are life. (John 6:63)

We remember to be aware of His ways and instruction, such that our hearts are etched with the Words of His law. Grow in Grace.... Meaning to grow in the knowledge of His forgiveness and remember His Words, as you celebrate His mercy and grace. In our growth, as followers of Yahshua (Jesus), we need to keep our eyes on Him and stay hooked to Him ....The door. Inside The door to the Father's house is the kingdom of God, where righteousness is the norm.

Mat 6:33 But seek ye first the kingdom of God, and his righteousness; and all these things shall be added unto you.

# Devil / Daemon
# <u>Shed</u>

ד     שׁ

Dalet     Shin

<u>Door</u>     <u>Teeth</u>
Entrance    Destroy

## Destroy The Door

Ps 106:37   Yea, they sacrificed their sons and their daughters unto <u>devils</u>,

The Door to the Father's house is the Door to life.  His house is about life now and life eternal.  The Word is the Door of the Son and the Door of the Shepherd's covenant.  The devil is against everything and anything that has to do with God's Word, correctly described in the letters, Shin, Dalet; "Destroy The Door".   The devil wants to destroy the Door to life that we are hooked to by faith.  The whole mission of the devil is to get us off the path of righteousness and to destroy the Door to God's kingdom.

The devil is against life.  He promotes chaos, destruction, devastation, and ultimately anything that promotes death.  The devil is the enemy of righteousness and perverts life. (Acts 13:10)

The Word of God is the basis for our reasoning, logic, thought, ideas, philosophy and theology, etc. This is why the devil (shed) is against everything found in the Word (Dabar); Door of The Son. In the parable re: the Seed, being the Word of God, one can see that the devil looks to take the Word out of one's heart, so they will not keep it, believe, be saved and bring forth fruit with patience. (Luke 8:10-15)

The devil is like a roaring lion and is always looking for someone to devour. (1 Pet 5:8) We overcome the temptations and wiles of the devil the same way Yahshua (Jesus) did, when he was tempted to sin. Yahshua stated that man does not live by bread alone, but by every Word (Bread of life) that proceeds from the mouth of God. (Mat 4:1-4) Our connection to protection is through the Word of God, as His Words are Spirit and they are life. We put on the armor of God, with the sword of the Spirit. (Eph 6:11-17)

By being hooked to the Door, the Word of God, we submit ourselves to Him, following His ways, knowing that His Word is Truth. (John 17:15-17) In doing this, we discover and understand the best way to resist the devil and to stay connected to our LORD. The devil will then flee from us, as we stay connected to our source of strength. The devil wants to destroy the Door, the source of our strength, the Word of God.

James 4:7  Submit yourselves therefore to God. Resist the devil, and he will flee from you.

## Hate / Enemy
## <u>Sane</u>

| א | נ | שׂ |
|---|---|---|
| Aleph | Nun | Shin |
| Ox | Fish | Teeth |
| <u>Ox</u> | <u>Fish</u> | <u>Teeth</u> |
| Strength | Life | Destroy |

## Destroy Life's Strength / Power

Prov 8:35-36   For whoso findeth me findeth life, and shall obtain favour of the LORD.  But he that sinneth against me wrongeth his own soul: all they that hate me love death.

Yahshua the Messiah (Jesus) came that we would have life and have it more abundantly. (John 10:10)  Anything against life is destroying life's strength and shows ones attitude toward death.  Hate is counter to life and promotes chaos, leading to curses and eventually death.  We have been admonished to choose who we will serve.  In choosing the LORD, we find blessings and life.  When choosing other gods, we find curses, and death becomes our eternal destiny.  (Deut 30: 15-20)

Our strength is not found in hate, but in love.  Love is the greatest gift given to us by our

Creator. We become a partner with Him, while we support anything that has to do with promoting life and uplifting His creation. Love is the foundation of His design for the world. When we walk in the Spirit, we reveal Him living in us through the fruit of the Spirit. The greatest of these fruits being love. (1Cor 13:13) We express Him living in us, when we show love. After all, God is love, and when one has God dwelling in them, God will perfect His love in their lives, as they grow and nurture their faith. (1John 4:11-16)

One can hate the things that are against the LORD and against life, but hating life is not in harmony with His kingdom. Hating whatever is evil and opposed to life is supporting the essence of life and the LORD's whole purpose in creation. We are His children and followers of His Way, and what creation is all about.

Loving the LORD, His righteousness, and hating iniquity, supports the notion that we are against whatever destroys life's strength. Hate is the enemy of life and results in being the enemy of our faith; faith nurtures life. The Messiah called us out of the world and warned us that we would be hated by the world, because we choose to follow Him. Hate and evil are against life.

John 15:19  If ye were of the world, the world would love his own: but because ye are not of the world, but I have chosen you out of the world, therefore the world hateth you.

# Walk / Come
# Halak

ד ל ה

Kaf — Lamed — Hey

Palm / Bless — Staff / Shepherd — Hands Raised / Reveal

## Behold / Reveal The Shepherd's Blessing

Ps 84:11   For the LORD God is a sun and shield: the LORD will give grace and glory: no good thing will he withhold from them that walk uprightly.

When we walk with the LORD, in beholding Him, we reveal His blessings, because we are seeking to follow His Words, not doctrines of men, or the imaginations of our own hearts. As we walk with Him, the inevitable results are the blessings He bestows upon us. Beholding and revealing is a "two way" street. Staying focused on Him, beholding Him, automatically creates within us the desire and ability to reveal Him in our lives, because we walk together with Him.

By beholding Him in our daily walk, we become changed. As His Spirit reveals the LORD to us, we find liberty. While walking in the Spirit, we grow into the image He intended for us from the beginning. We were originally created in the image of God, and now, due to the "fall", we need His light to guide us in our walk, because we have been blinded by the god of this world. (2 Cor 3:17-18) (Gen 1:27) (2 Cor 4:4)

When walking with Him we find true freedom. Freedom comes not from the wisdom of this world, but from His Words and precepts. (Ps 119:45)  The things he asks us to do are for our own good.   Walking with Him is walking in the Spirit.  Living in the Spirit is a step by step journey through life, beholding Him and revealing Him in our actions, and not fulfilling the lusts of the flesh.  (Gal 5:16, 25)

In beholding Him we find light and we are able to see the truth.  In Him is the way to walk, the reality of truth, and the life we should be living. We reveal Him to the world through our witness, and our witness reveals the blessings our Shepherd has for us to share.  The blessings of the fruit of the Spirit will emanate from our being as we practice love, joy, peace, longsuffering, gentleness, goodness, faith, meekness, and temperance.  (Gal 5:22-23)

Walking with Him is a conscious resolve to keep our minds beholding The Shepherd of our lives. Walk and learn of Him and witness His blessing.

Col 1:10   That ye might walk worthy of the Lord unto all pleasing, being fruitful in every good work, and increasing in the knowledge of God.

# Answer / Hear
## <u>Anah</u>

| ה | נ | ע |
|---|---|---|
| Hey | Nun | Ayin |
| 👤 | ↘ | 👁 |
| <u>Hands Raised</u> | <u>Fish</u> | <u>Eye</u> |
| Reveal | Life | See |

## See Life Revealed

Ps 69:13   But as for me, my prayer is unto thee, O LORD, in an acceptable time: O God, in the multitude of thy mercy <u>hear</u> me, in the truth of thy salvation.

The LORD will answer our prayers in His timing, consistent with the truth that is in harmony with His saving mercy.  He will hear and answer us according to His will.  (1 John 5:14) We see life revealed to us, as we walk with Him, for His answers are always revealed to us through our connection with life.

Answers are shown to us, after they are heard, but first, the request must be made.  Yahshua (Jesus) told us to ask and it shall be given to us, seek and you shall find, and to knock and it shall be opened to us.  (Mat 7:7)  The key factor for us is to trust in and to make our requests known to

Him. He will always give an answer. If the request does not come to pass, it might be delayed, or the answer might be a "no", because it is not in harmony with His plan.

The answer is always found in beholding life. Life is the ultimate priority in our existence on earth. The whole ultimate plan of salvation is to rescue us from death. Life in the present and eternal life in the future is the definitive answer to everything. The answers that emerge from The LORD are always pursuant to life, whether in the short term or the long term. All things work together for good and the LORD weaves it all together, when we trust and acknowledge Him, as can be seen throughout the Scriptures. (Rom 8:28; Gen 50:20; Prov 3:5-6)

Our lives are the answer to the hope that is within us. We live out our lives, as the response to our faith. The prayer of Yahshua (Jesus), The Messiah, was "thy kingdom come, thy will be done on earth, as it is in heaven". His prayer was for us to see life, His kingdom, revealed in us. We do this by following and sharing His Word, by revealing the Spirit of His Kingdom in our hearts. Upon hearing His Word, the answer to His prayer is life, according to His design, revealed to us, through us, and to others.

1 Peter 3:15 But sanctify the LORD God in your hearts: and be ready always to give an answer to every man that asketh you a reason of the hope that is in you with meekness and fear:

# Miracle / Wonderful
## Pala

| א | ל | פ |
|---|---|---|
| Aleph | Lamed | Pey |
| Ox | Staff | Mouth |
| Power | Shepherd | Voice |

### The Voice with The Shepherd's Power

Ps 107:8  Oh that men would praise the LORD for his goodness, and for his <u>wonderful</u> works to the children of men! (see vs.15, 21, 31)

The voice of the shepherd produces miracles for us to realize the power of His Words. From the beginning of creation He performed wonders to reveal His power and might. Many of these miracles we take for granted, because we have seen the wonders of His creation since birth. We need to stop, stand still, and consider the marvels of His design. (Job 37:14)

Do you wonder where all of "this" came from? The scriptures clearly say that He created the heavens by His Word and the breath of His mouth. The heavens declare His glory and His handiwork. (Ps 33:6; Ps 19:1) The voice of His power is beyond words for us to explain, and is fittingly and "simply" described as a miracle. "And God said" is a quote mentioned many, many times throughout the Scriptures. Each day of creation He used this phrase proving the awesome power of His voice. We need to speak often of the glorious honor of His majesty and wondrous works in our lives. (Ps 145:5)

The 29th Psalm shares with us the LORD's power and strength. His power is identified to us through His voice. His voice impacts the world we live, in many ways. We worship the LORD, because of who He is, and for the related glory only He can create for us to recognize through His voice. He is powerful, full of majesty, holy, and He will give strength to those that follow Him, who are called by His name, His people. In following Him, He will bless with the peace of His glorious design; the peace, only He can offer.

The complete actuality of His wonder and marvellous works will be realized at the culmination of all things, at the time of the end. We will witness His glory and see the fulfilment of His plan of salvation. The reality of His truth will be verified to us in a magnificent way, as we witness His miraculous grandeur. We will not be able to hold back from praising Him.

Rev 15:3 And they sing the song of Moses the servant of God, and the song of the Lamb, saying, Great and marvellous are thy works Lord God Almighty; just and true are thy ways, thou King of saints.

# Error / Astray / Wander
## Ta`ah

ה ע ת

Hey — Ayin — Tav

👤 👁 †

Hands Raised — Eye — Cross
Revealed — Understand — Covenant

## Covenant Understanding Revealed

Isaiah 53:6 All we like sheep have gone astray; we have turned every one to his own way; and the LORD hath laid on him the iniquity of us all.

Like Adam and Eve we have chosen to go our own way. The "good news" is that the LORD has provided us with the covenant of life to follow. The decision not to follow is wandering into the covenant of chaos, leading to death. The LORD has provided us with the covenant of life through His redemption; the Way, the Truth and the Life. (John 14:6) To see and live in His covenant reveals the true blessings found in life.

When one continues to follow after other gods, by ignoring the voice of the LORD, and refusing to understand the ways of the Creator, he chooses by his actions, to remain astray in the congregation (church) of the dead. (Prov 21:16)

To ignore the covenant with life and to be seduced by other influences is a constant theme found throughout the Bible for us to understand. Understanding the covenant and living in covenant with the LORD is paramount to living a life of blessing, for He has come that we would have an abundant life. (John 10:10) He has counseled us throughout the Scriptures to follow Him in the covenant life and not to wander or stray after other gods, leading us into chaos, curses and ultimately death. (Deut 30:19-20)

The light of God will help us to see and lead us through life. His light is the only source of truth, revealing an accurate perspective of His covenant principles, which is vital to experiencing the blessings He has waiting for us. Walking with Him we enter the covenant of life.

Yahshua (Jesus) said that His sheep hear His voice and they follow Him. In following Him we do our best to live out the principles He has taught us. By joining with our Shepherd, we reveal Him to the world. The evidence of this behavior will be perceived and revealed in the fruit of what we think, say and do. If one does not hear His voice, ignores Him and wanders away, that one has gone astray and has chosen to follow the spirit of error.

1 John 4:6   We are of God: he that knoweth God heareth us; he that is not of God heareth not us. Hereby know we the spirit of truth, and the spirit of error.

# False / Falsehood / Lies
## Sheger

| ר | ק | שׁ |
|---|---|---|
| Resh | Kof | Shin |

| Head | Back of Head | Teeth |
|---|---|---|
| Man | Follow | Destroy |

## Destruction Following Man

Jer 13:25   This is thy lot, the portion of thy measures from me, saith the LORD; because thou hast forgotten me, and trusted in falsehood.

Destruction follows ones thoughts, if the thoughts are not based on truth. The LORD is all about what is real, not what is false.   Lies and falsehood generates error, confusion, and destruction in the world around us. The Holy Spirit positively guides our thoughts, impacting our emotions, and eventually motivates our actions. Actions based on lies will create more negative results, leading to chaos, and over time, compounding into destruction and death.

The creation is established and based on the laws of nature. The laws of nature form the reality of His creation and embody the truths of life. A falsehood is to look upon His laws in a negative context, as His laws are for our good. His laws represent the way He wants us to understand and interact with His reality, where blessings follow your thoughts, because your thoughts and actions are based on His words. His words are true and not false concepts leading to ruin. Even one of the Ten Commandments expresses the concept not to bear false witness and is included in the New Covenant, written on our hearts. (Jer 31:33) Chaos and destruction is the only product of falsehood and life cannot be perpetuated with deception of any kind.

We are admonished not to follow false prophets and not to be lured by their apparent miracles, signs and wonders. If they speak not according to His word, there is no light in them, and we should avoid following after their falsehood. The scriptures warn us to make sure that what we follow as principles for life are supported by the word of God. We must follow the light of His word and not remain in the error of darkness. (Isaiah 8: 20-22) Trouble and destruction follow ones thoughts, if those thoughts are not united to truth, God's word. His words are spirit and they are life. (John 6:63) Living life His way is living in the truth, not falsehood. Stay in the truth and good things will follow you, not destruction.

1 John 4:1   Beloved, believe not every spirit, but try the spirits whether they are of God: because many false prophets have gone out into the world.

# Shepherd / Feed / Pastor
## Ra`ah

| ה | ע | ר |
|---|---|---|
| Hey | Ayin | Resh |

| Hands Raised | Eye | Head |
|---|---|---|
| Reveal | Understand | Man |

## Man's Understanding Revealed

Ps 23:1 A Psalm of David. The LORD is my shepherd; I shall not want.

Man's understanding of life is revealed by whom he or she is following. We follow the voice of the shepherd and feed with the flock that shares the same discernment. The voice of the Good Shepherd is the voice that is consistent with the words found in the Scriptures. The LORD said that His sheep hear His voice and they follow Him. (John 10:27)

Beholding a voice and following a shepherd sets the stage for what we are being fed. We need to know the source of what the shepherd is feeding us and make sure it is the Bread of life from the Good Shepherd. (John 6:33-35) We need to verify that the bread we are eating is truly the Bread from heaven that will give us eternal life.

Another key to following the True Shepherd is to make sure we enter the sheepfold through the door. Any shepherd must enter through the door the LORD as provided. If a shepherd enters into the sheepfold to tend to the sheep any other way, he should not be followed. (John 10:1-14)

Our understanding must be that all shepherds and pastors need to be in line with His Word in order to be true leaders and pastors of the flock. We must make sure that we are taught according to the word of the True Shepherd. The Scriptures tell us that man's understanding and teaching is essential to be according to the law and the testimony of Scripture, or else there is no light in them. (Ish 8:20) We reveal to the world what we have come to know and understand. We must be vigilant to make sure our understanding is in harmony with Him and that we teach others in the flock to grow in His everlasting principles. (2Cor 3:18)

The shepherd will inspire you to do the right things, because his understanding of life in the Spirit is consistent with what was written to us.

Heb 13:20-21 Now the God of peace, that brought again from the dead our Lord Jesus, that great shepherd of the sheep, through the blood of the everlasting covenant, Make you perfect in every good work to do his will, working in you that which is wellpleasing in his sight, through Jesus Christ; to whom be glory for ever and ever. Amen

## Sustain / Nourish / Feed
## Kuwl

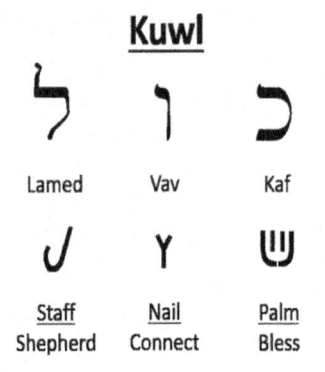

| ל | ו | כ |
|---|---|---|
| Lamed | Vav | Kaf |
| ∫ | Y | ⊔ |
| <u>Staff</u> | <u>Nail</u> | <u>Palm</u> |
| Shepherd | Connect | Bless |

### Blessings Connected to The Shepherd

Ps 55:22   Cast thy burden upon the LORD, and he shall <u>sustain</u> thee: he shall never suffer the righteous to be moved.

The Shepherd's open hand of blessing is always there for us to connect with and hold. He wants us to be secured with Him to realize all of the blessings of life that are available to us. The more we stay connected to Him, the more we will experience His "Godsend". His Ways are integral to and operate within the revelation of the blessing. The blessed life that He wants us to experience is revealed in following His way and truth. (John 14:6) When living His way, we experience the blessings and reality He created.

As we partake of His word and put His wisdom into action, the expected result will be a wholesome, beautiful, and fulfilling life. His word nurtures us when we heed the faith and follow the good doctrine, as revealed in the Word of God. (1 Tim 4:6) Similar to our physical health for eating healthy and living in harmony with the laws of nature, He created our spiritual life with principles that will bring about an abundant reality. (John 10:10) When we stay connected to Him with a healthy spiritual diet, we are nourished, as we are fed with the bread of life.

The LORD said that He would keep us in perfect peace, as we stay connected to Him in our thoughts. (Isaiah 26:3) In addition to studying His word, He want us to live attached to Him, as we live out our lives on a moment by moment basis, with Him as our source for answers in life. Even in the hard times, He will sustain us and provide, as we stay joined to Him. (Neh 9:20-21)

All throughout the Scriptures it is evident that The LORD takes care of His people through "thick and thin". During the future time of trouble and in the great tribulation, the key for anyone to be protected and rescued is to stay connected to The Shepherd. Eventual blessings come amid the hard times, when we stay attached to Him. He will feed us and will lead us to the fountain of livings waters, as He is that fountain of everlasting life. (John 4:13-14)

Rev 7:17  For the lamb which is in the midst of the throne shall feed them, and shall lead them unto living fountains of waters: and God shall wipe away all tears from their eyes.

## Table / Tablet
## Luwach

| ח | ו | ל |
|---|---|---|
| Chet | Vav | Lamed |
| 𒑱 (Wall) | Y (Nail) | J (Staff) |
| **Wall** | **Nail** | **Staff** |
| Protect | Connect | Shepherd |

## The Shepherd's Connection for Protection

Prov 7:1-3  My son, keep my words, and lay up my commandments with thee.  Keep my commandments, and live; and my law as the apple of thine eye.  Bind them upon thy fingers, write them upon the <u>table</u> of thine heart.

The Shepherd of our house lives in our heart. (h. Lev)  Our connection with The Shepherd is found on the table of our heart.  Everything we choose to do is based on our "heart knowledge". We learn and understand "head knowledge", but the application of our knowledge comes from our heart, and is what we truly believe.  Studying the Word and allowing The LORD to write the truth of His words on our heart is one of the most important things we can do, if not, <u>the</u> most important thing we can do in life.  (Prov 3:3) The table of the heart is our connection to the new covenant.  He will write His Law in our hearts, He will be our God and we shall be His people. (Jer 31:31-34) We will want to follow His ways, and commandments, because of our desire to have a relationship with Him. Our desire to please Him will be because we love Him, not because we have to earn His love. His grace is our strength to live in covenant with Him, and if we sin, and confess our sins, it is His grace again that provides our forgiveness and will cleanse us from all unrighteousness, as we grow in grace. (1John 1:9; 2Pet 3:18)

When we come to Him, He will give us a new heart, where He will communicate and write His Word for us to follow. His Spirit will live in us, after He takes the stony heart out of our flesh. He told us that His Words are Spirit and His Words are life. (Ez 36:26-27; John 6:63)

As we experience our lives with The Messiah living in us (Eph 3:16-19), we are to be as living letters, messages from God. With the Spirit living in us, we are the temple of God, and we must represent Him to the world with our fruit, in what we think, say and do. (1 Cor 3:16-17) The Shepherd and The Spirit connect us to the protection we need, as our heart is shepherding our house, where He writes to us on our tablet.

2 Cor 3:3 Forasmuch as ye are manifestly declared to be the epistle of Christ ministered by us, written not with ink, but with the Spirit of the living God; not in tables of stone, but in fleshly tables of the heart.

# Mercy / Kindness / Merciful
## Checed

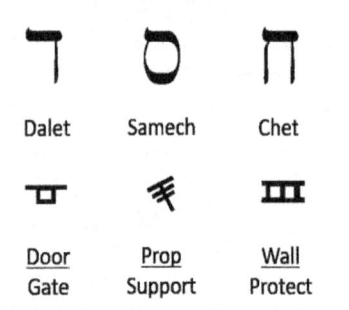

ד     ס     ח

Dalet    Samech    Chet

Door     Prop     Wall
Gate     Support    Protect

## Protection Depending upon The Door

Ps 23:6  Surely goodness and <u>mercy</u> shall follow me all the days of my life: and I will dwell in the house of the LORD for ever.

Mercy follows us in life, as we depend on Him in all things. We come into the Father's house through the door, Yahshua (Jesus).(John 10:7-9) He provides protection to us in many ways and supports us in times of need and trouble.

It is very important to understand the readiness of the LORD to forgive us when we call upon Him. (Ps 86:5-6) When it comes to how He attends to our supplications, He has us protected in two ways; with mercy and/or grace. Being deserving of the consequences of our sins, we find mercy.

We also should conduct our lives with mercy, as

a basic fundamental requirement of our walk with the LORD.  He has told us to do justly, walk humbly and love mercy.  (Micah 6:8)  These attributes are essential ingredients of His kingdom and necessary for our walk with Him.  Compassion is paramount in His House, especially when we enter through the Door that provides and represents mercy in our lives.

The LORD is faithful to us when we cry out to Him for mercy and forgiveness.  We lean on Him and depend on Him daily to be merciful to us.  (Ps 86:3-4)  Our prayers in the Spirit are the vehicle for our communications with Him.

The examples given to us in scripture illustrate our need to come humbly unto Him and admit our sins to the LORD.  (Luke 18:13-14)  He does not want us to be exalted in our relationship with Him, but He wants us to be humble in His mercy toward us.  His mercy and grace provides the forgiveness we need to grow beyond our life of justification and into our life of sanctification.

Simply said:  Mercy is not getting the penalty we deserve and grace is getting the reward we don't deserve.  This clarifies our need to fully depend upon The Door for our Salvation.  He will provide the mercy we need, because we can boldly trust and rely on Him for our needed protection.

Hebrews 4:16   Let us therefore come boldly unto the throne of grace, that we may obtain mercy, and find grace to help in time of need.

# Testimony / Witness
## `Edah

| הֵ | ד | ע |
|---|---|---|
| Hey | Dalet | Ayin |

| 🙌 | ⊓ | 👁 |
|---|---|---|
| Hands Raised | Door | Eye |
| Reveal | Gate | See |

## See The Door Revealed

Ps 25:10  All the paths of the LORD are mercy and truth unto such as keep his covenant and his <u>testimonies</u>.

We truly witness when we put our thoughts and understanding into action.  The results solidify our testimony.  When we put our understanding of The LORD into practice, we become a witness through the power of His testimony in us.  As we reveal the Word of God in our lives, we live out the Way, the Truth and the Life.  (John 14:6) We are to be doers of the Word and not hearers only (James 1:22-25).  The Word, being the Door of the Son, is the very truth we need to understand, in order to be effective witnesses for Him.  We see how our testimony is revealed, when we enter the Father's house, through the Door, and put His Words into action in our lives. Our testimony and witness is revealing the Door.

Once we reveal the Door, we are living inside the Father's House, in His Kingdom. As you internalize the Words of Scripture and letters in this devotional, they will become part of your thought process and you will live with the Words living in you. You will grow, as a testimony to His Word, and your life will be presented: a witness for Him. In doing that, others will see the Door revealed to them. They will want to enter, due to your life witness and testimony.

Our witness is the evidence and testimony of what we believe. When we believe in the Son of God, we have the witness living within us and we have the gift of eternal life. (1John 5:1-13) Since we have the gift of eternal life, we live life in that context and are witnesses, living and walking in the fruit of the Spirit. (Gal 5:22-26)

This being the last word in this devotional, it is appropriate for our witness to be strong during the end times. Without predicting the day or the hour, the final events of the last days mentioned in the Scriptures are getting closer and closer. In the latter days, those that reveal their behavior with the testimony of the Messiah, will be at war with the worldly powers at that time. We must continue to be a strong witness, by revealing the Door to the Father's house. Shalom !!!

Rev 12:17 And the dragon was wroth with the woman, and went to make war with the remnant of her seed, which keep the commandments of God, and have the testimony of Jesus Christ.

Meditate on these words and letters during the day ….. see His Word and Letters come alive in your heart.